UNAPOLOGETIC
WORK LIFE BALANCE

A Corporate Warrior's Guide to Creating
the Life You Love at Work and Home

JANINE GRAZIANO-FULL, CPCC

BALBOA.PRESS
A DIVISION OF HAY HOUSE

Copyright © 2020 Janine Graziano-Full, CPCC.

All rights reserved. No part of this book may be used or reproduced by any means, graphic, electronic, or mechanical, including photocopying, recording, taping or by any information storage retrieval system without the written permission of the author except in the case of brief quotations embodied in critical articles and reviews.

Balboa Press books may be ordered through booksellers or by contacting:

Balboa Press
A Division of Hay House
1663 Liberty Drive
Bloomington, IN 47403
www.balboapress.com
844-682-1282

Because of the dynamic nature of the Internet, any web addresses or links contained in this book may have changed since publication and may no longer be valid. The views expressed in this work are solely those of the author and do not necessarily reflect the views of the publisher, and the publisher hereby disclaims any responsibility for them.

The author of this book does not dispense medical advice or prescribe the use of any technique as a form of treatment for physical, emotional, or medical problems without the advice of a physician, either directly or indirectly. The intent of the author is only to offer information of a general nature to help you in your quest for emotional and spiritual well-being. In the event you use any of the information in this book for yourself, which is your constitutional right, the author and the publisher assume no responsibility for your actions.

Print information available on the last page.

Cover Photo by Janine Graziano-Full.
Author Photo by Renee Dee Photography.
Cover Design by Amy Suzanne Taggart.

ISBN: 978-1-9822-5626-5 (sc)
ISBN: 978-1-9822-5628-9 (hc)
ISBN: 978-1-9822-5627-2 (e)

Library of Congress Control Number: 2020919665

Balboa Press rev. date: 10/30/2020

For Nick, Olivia, Ray and Elizabeth,
the most important reasons why I
unapologetically balance my life.

CONTENTS

Forewords ix
Introduction xvii

Chapter 1   Mirror, Mirror 1
Chapter 2   Revolution 5
Chapter 3   Evolution 15
Chapter 4   You Are Here 21
Chapter 5   The Path to Powerful Choices 37
Chapter 6   Defining and Living Your Values 49
Chapter 7   You Are the Boss of You 59
Chapter 8   Your Best Co-pilot 75
Chapter 9   Your Unapologetic Life 85
Chapter 10 LEADERship 97
Chapter 11 "Thriveability" 113

Resources 119
Acknowledgments 121
About the Author 125
Thank You 127

FOREWORDS

Meet Janine

By Bob Gamgort, Executive Chairman
and CEO - Keurig Dr Pepper

Flash back to 15 years ago: I'm a newly promoted president for the North American portfolio of a large consumer products company, with 12 direct reports across the U.S., Canada and Mexico. This was my greatest leadership challenge to date, but it also threatened my ability to maintain balance in my life, as the workload, travel and stress compromised the quantity and quality of family time and "me" time. To ease the transition, I asked HR to assign someone to help with "team effectiveness" — a staffer who could help prepare the leadership team agenda, ensure we were ready for our meetings and capture and facilitate the follow-ups to our agreed actions.

This is when I met Janine. As a young HR manager who had spent most of her career in R&D and procurement, she seemed like an unlikely candidate for our team effectiveness resource. But her ideas for the role, fearlessness in dealing with senior leaders and infectious positive energy led me to make a bet on her. Her ability to make the complex simple and cut though all of the "noise" as she distilled key conclusions and necessary follow-ups made her remarkably effective in the role. She also embraced the high-performance team (HPT) process, holding us accountable not just for our "to-do" list, but also for our behaviors and working style as a team. Over time she took her HPT thinking to a broader level, considering the "whole person," not just the "work person," which caused me to rethink some of my priorities as well.

At the end of her assignment, Janine asked me for career advice. I told her that she had the unique ability to be an executive coach, either inside or outside of the organization, and she should follow her passion. Later, when she launched her own coaching business I became one of her first clients and have worked with her ever since, recommending her to key players in my organization. I'm proud of her for having the courage to create a career that balances her professional and personal needs, impressed with her dedication to help others reach the same goal and honored to be asked to write the foreword to her book.

This book represents the best of Janine's thinking. Don't be deceived by the length as it's densely packed with the concepts, tools and frameworks she uses in her practice. My advice is to read through the book once, to understand the overall concepts, and return to those that meet your needs at that moment. You will likely find that as your situation evolves, you'll want to go back to some of the other tools and frameworks. Keep a notebook nearby, as the book will spark a number of important thoughts that you'll want to capture and work on later.

I'll close with the saying "trust the process." Speaking from experience, while it's not easy to dedicate the time and energy to focus on yourself and be intentional about the journey, doing so can have a remarkable impact on your life satisfaction and positively impact others around you. While far from being a role model for "life balance," I'm happy to report that by working with Janine and employing many of the concepts in this book, I am making progress every day.

Bob Gamgort
(Business executive, husband, father, son, family member and friend)

What Work Life Balance Means

By Cy Wakeman, author and trainer and founder of Reality Based Leadership

The number one question I get asked when I am on the road speaking in front of a group of people is "how do you do it all?"

And my answer? "Pretty effortlessly, joyfully, willingly, intentionally, and while at peace." (Now I will add to that answer: "unless I forget to practice all the strategies that Janine provides to us in her fabulous book, *Unapologetic Work Life Balance: A Corporate Warrior's Guide to Creating the Life You Love at Work*!")

Why this question so often? People truly wonder if I have some secret to being happy even when life is messy or very full. I have a few things going on in my life. I am married, I have four sons and four stepsons — eight sons between the ages of 14 and 27. I have been a single mother. I am a founder and CEO of a multi-million dollar company, I am a boss, I travel four to five days a week, and am usually in a different city each day. I research, I have written three books, one a *New York Times* bestseller. I am an influencer on social media and am prolific on many channels, I have a popular podcast, I read a lot, I hang out with friends, I care for family members, I travel to very cool places on vacation, I mentor others, I volunteer, and I sleep and enjoy downtime.

All of these things are the results of how I have learned to live. It just isn't about the doing — you are capable of great things when you are doing them in service to others without harm to yourself.

I am grateful that I discovered long ago that "work life balance" is a *verb*. It is not a noun; not a future state or even a fleeting moment of having it all. It isn't about doing more or having more. It isn't anything external. The more I focus externally, the farther away I move from what it really is. Work life balance is a set of actions I take and choices I make based on information I gather in my internal world through a practice of self-reflection and meditation. It is about managing my energy, not time, nor tasks, nor to-do lists. It is about tuning in and managing my energy away from what depletes me spiritually and towards what is spirit building for me. Having clarity about what I value and a keen sense of how my energy is affected by my current choices, along with an intermittent glimpse at why I am on this planet, creates a recipe for moving through life giving freely and many times effortlessly. Energy is how I measure whether I am on track, aligned and choosing well.

I am no saint and I am not any more enlightened than any of you who have picked up this book hoping that you can create the life you love. I haven't "arrived," as there is no destination. I have to actively balance my life; I stumble, get off track and have to recalibrate. I screw this up, but only daily. Perfection isn't the point, either: it is all about progress, readjustments and self-compassion.

My current approach to living a life on purpose is the accumulation of 54 years of trial and error, learning from those painful moments, such as when my choices had me giving energy to work rather than being with my mom as she passed because I didn't want to "let someone down." So much wisdom was given to me by the amazing women in my life who have gone before, along with lots of coaching from extraordinary life coaches and teachers.

It's a lifetime collection of strategies, exercises for self-reflection, adjustments, and heart to hearts with my family.

That is why I am so excited to endorse Janine's fabulous work in this book. She gives you the most amazing gift — the process, strategies and techniques by which you can do a great reality-check in your life. And when you have insight, when you know better, you can be better, do better, and feel better.

I am honored to write this foreword. As I mentioned, it is all about energy for me. When I first met Janine, that is what struck me about her — her amazing energy. She was joyful, focused, accountable, in charge of her own happiness, and on a mission to help people create more lovely lives according to their own design. Her energy and joy were striking, really. I paid attention as she was one of those people I meet who seemed to be actually living her values out loud in the moment, not privately, after hours, in her spare time. Her beliefs and techniques aligned with Reality-Based Leadership and all that we teach, especially our core message: that suffering is optional and most often self-imposed.

I am confident you will enjoy Janine's beautiful provocation in this book, pushing you to claim what you want, no longer apologizing for designing the life you feel great in. Her stories are both funny and too familiar to me — work, breast pumps, crazy schedules and unfortunately that horrid feeling, as my head hit the pillow, of a loved one's chronic disappointment in me. I so related to the time in my life that I was called to figure out a different way to move through life, more skillfully. When I learned that what you give attention to determines that quality of your life — that was a big lesson for me.

Janine will take you through a journey to help you take your life back, one precious minute at a time, so you can kick ass at work and life and everywhere you want. Isn't that a great promise? Work your way through this book and actually do the exercises for self-reflection, not intellectually bypassing, but really settling in and meditating over her big, beautiful questions. If you dare, you will be able to strike a balance that feeds all parts of you. While you may not be able to have it all, you can find a mix in which you can love it all. Use your curiosity non-judgmentally to evolve. Let your values be your guide. Try out the great techniques and see what changes; test and adapt, often.

You have in your hands the makings of a great reality check. A habit of successful, happy people is that they check in, get aware, accept what they have come to realize about themselves and use that knowledge to evolve a bit and to fuel their choices and their happiness.

Again, this is not something you can learn once and check off your "to-do" list. This is an on-going ritual to add into your life. You will need to adjust as you grow, as your life changes, as you know more. Feel pain or stress? Simply self-reflect, get aware, accept, self-forgive, and, calmly and neutrally, begin again with a powerful choice. It is such a peaceful formula for a wonderful life without regrets.

My current mantra as I walk through life? "Cy, do only that which you can do in peace." I am currently curating my life to only include on my list that which I can do and remain in peace, living up to the person I want to be — only doing what I can do peacefully, joyfully, willingly, on purpose, intentionally, which by definition for me is how I know I am answering my calling in this life. It's not about what I accomplish or get done but about how it feels to be aligned with Source.

And know that you can't ace this test — yep, no final grade is given. It is about the process and the practice so ... stay curious and stay compassionate. Good enough is good enough — because you are good enough. The universe is kind and fills in all around us all that we need. And in case you are trying to go it alone, reading this book and "fixing" your own life: Don't take the hard road. Look for the helpers. There are always helpers. When you can, be a helper. We are not alone, and we got this. You are a peaceful warrior. I promise, even if you don't feel it in this moment, you are a peaceful warrior in the making.

INTRODUCTION

Here you are, reading the very beginning of our written-word journey together. Perhaps this is the first exposure you have to me, and you are coming in hoping for a shift in your world. Or maybe you already know me from my professional or personal circle, and you are also hoping for a shift in your world. Either way, welcome to the pages!

I already sense many an eyebrow raising in response to the title of this book, "Unapologetic Work Life Balance." I've even been told by several people that "there is no work life balance." Work is a part of life, and you'll never be in sync with everything all the time. There are movements out there that use phrases such as work life harmony, work life integration, etc., all of which intend to be of service in the same way: more synergy, Zen, fun and fulfillment and less dichotomy, chaos, stress and burnout. And while we could be moving towards more acceptance of the end game of harmony and synergy, in those dark, last-straw moments of the week when you've had enough, I wonder what phrase you are Googling or saying to yourself most. The known "work life balance" is the common term, like it or not, and whether you are searching for balance, integration, synergy, etc., this path — striving for work life balance — is a beautiful provocation, pushing you to claim what you want, one step at a time, as you turn the pages of this book.

As for "unapologetic," my wish is for you to stop apologizing — both at work and at home — because you have a life or because you want a more fulfilling life. I understand that you show respect for others at work and at home by asking for permission, and likely still asking for forgiveness even when granted that permission. And yet, you were born into this world with dreams, missions and desires all of your own. It's time to reflect inward, listen hard to what your own story is, and stand for something without regret.

Whether you know me or not, here is a bit more about who I am and what I offer you in these pages. I was a corporate warrior, I am married to a corporate warrior, and I now coach corporate warriors. I've been called to serve the willing warriors by coaching them to increase their awareness, tame their stressors and assist them in making powerful choices to create a holistic life they love. I was moved to leave my corporate career to be a coach so that you don't have to leave yours. I still have stress and am at times overwhelmed. I, too, am a client of my own processes. This book shares the compilation of what I have learned both in and out of the corporate world, from others and from life experience. I've developed these lessons to provide you with perspective and tools to break through any burnout and live your best life.

My hope is that, as you read this, you feel as if you are having a drink with me and we are chatting about these examples and tools. It's an invitation to a conversation in service of you. You'll be more prepared to navigate choppy waters and enjoy the smooth sailing, no matter how briefly or long either lasts.

At this point in time, I provide coaching services to a few companies, which can be very rewarding when that work results in loyalty, trust, relationships and results over time. Yet, at the same time, I feel my reach is skinny, rather than wide, and I know that my impact is more limited than it could be. This book helps me help more people by offering a comprehensive compilation of the "Janine-isms" and wisdom nuggets that I share with my clients and that I've learned from others I've met along the way. You may have heard concepts similar to some contained in this book before — whether in leadership books, in self-help books, through coaching or perhaps from reading about the Law of Attraction. My intention is to pull these ideas and others together and provide my own perspective; this book is a synthesis of learnings that I have used for myself and have been using with clients for over ten years.

On a personal note, I am honored to have a piece of me on a shelf for my children, family, friends, and clients to make use of when I'm long gone. I've had a vision for as long as I can remember of being a published author. I felt it was important for me to create a manual, guide, or compass of sorts to capture the state when I was in the flow of servant leadership and able to help as many people as possible. The book I saw myself writing would be not only a window into my world but also a service to my clients. In it, I would facilitate a conversation between me and my ideal reader — a written coaching session in which I pull out of readers the struggles and fears my clients often experience and inspire them to live their best life. If I had died before publishing this book, it would truly have been one of my biggest regrets. And while I don't like to be motivated by fear, this is nonetheless important information to remind me what I really care about. We aren't getting out of this world alive. As I see it, I'm on this same journey you are. Now that you know a bit more about me, what is it that's calling you forth to live your best life? Let's turn the page and begin this journey together.

CHAPTER 1
MIRROR, MIRROR

The familiar but unwelcome buzz of the alarm goes off on your smartphone. It's Monday morning already?! The weekend went way too quickly. That's funny, what weekend? You worked most of it, anyway, catching up on emails and finishing that presentation for the upcoming board meeting. But at least you weren't actually in the office.

You are feeling some regret for not doing that workout you planned with your friend. This was the weekend you were going to get jump-started on some fitness routine. Oh well, there's always next weekend.

The list! Where is the list? There it is by the nightstand where you woke up a few times throughout the night trying to remember everything that you need to do this week. It looks impossibly long and very similar to last week's list — but it still needs to get done.

The morning routine is a full one. Feed yourself, feed your kids, pack the lunches (theirs, not yours … you eat takeout at your desk, if you eat lunch at all). Everyone has clean clothes on, although most of the laundry is still in piles. You *should* have time to take care of all this yourself, so you resist hiring some help.

The kids are delivered to school, and your morning commute begins. You start a phone call in transit to save some time. Bluetooth enabled (safety first), so you are hands-free and driving like a crazy person — navigating the lanes of other corporate warriors heading to the office.

The work call goes well, but it seems that deck you spent the weekend working on needs to be redone. Churn is a common theme in your world. You think: *Why is there always enough time to redo it, but never enough time to do it correctly during round one?*

Before you know it, you're at the office. You cruise for the usual spots, park, lock up, and head in. Another phone call comes in. You answer it, even though you know you are technically double-booked the moment you sit down at your desk. There is an emergency meeting called for 4:30 p.m. Weren't you supposed to leave early today for the kids' gymnastics double-practice tonight? Maybe you'll participate via phone on the commute home, or maybe you'll ask your neighbor to carpool again, even though it's your turn.

It's 9 a.m. on Monday morning, and it feels like you've lived nine lives already.

Time. Friend or foe? These days, there just isn't enough of it. You find yourself wishing for a few more hours in the day just to get it all done, or maybe for time to stand still altogether. Completing the items on your to-do list in a quality way is important to you. Who are we kidding … you basically strive for perfection. Your career is your focus, and that is a source of pride for you. But at what price?

Now, it seems normal to drag out office days longer, whether you are going in earlier or staying later. I mean, how else are you able to get it all done? That work isn't going to do itself. Sure, you have a team, but they are all buried as well, and you are the kind of jump-in-and-get-your-hands-dirty type that keeps everyone and everything afloat.

At home, though, the struggle is real. The list is just as long, and it's never done at the end of the day. The weekends are a good catch-up time, but you feel some additional hours during the workweek would make things easier as well. You think that there has to be a light at the end of the tunnel. Maybe you'll check off some boxes on your home list once you meet that upcoming work deadline.

Remember last time you thought, *once this is over, I can breathe. I'll have some space after the board meeting, after the presentation, after this deadline.* The thing is, there's always something else that creeps in. And you'll put your whole ass behind this deliverable, too, while the rest of your life feels half-assed.

Here we are again. Kicking ass at work, and half-assed everywhere else. It's getting old! You are teetering on the edge of burnout with no real parachute. Your career is so important to you. Not only is it a huge part of your identity, but it pays the bills and provides the benefits. And you've worked too hard and gotten too far to mess it up now.

This rock-star work ethic is admirable, but it's costing you your peace and happiness in other areas of your life. Maybe all other areas! Some days, it feels like you should jump on a jet plane to a remote island, chucking all electronics off the dock and into the water once you get there, never to look back.

Let's take a look at what all the pieces are to your dynamic life. You have work (we've established that all too well). Is it still fun for you? How fulfilling is it on a daily basis? Even though you spend eight hours (at the bare minimum, it's really more like 11+) working each day, there's more to you: You really are a dynamic human being with many facets, like a fine jewel.

We will take an in-depth look at all of these facets soon, but for now consider the following categories: career, money, health, romance/significant other, fun and recreation, family, friends, support system, personal development, physical environment, self-care, Higher Power/Higher Self. I bet one or many of these areas is suffering without your attention at the moment. This is not the time to judge yourself over this, but rather to just notice your truth (even if it's ugly).

This exercise is one of the first assessments I do with my clients when we coach together. Often, there are tears — either of surprise or just because of the mere validation of what they already knew. Once you assess the fulfillment, or lack thereof, in all areas of your life, you sometimes aren't happy with the truth in the moment. But now that they're here ... well, it's hard to un-see them. It's the ultimate rubbernecking with damaged parts of yourself all around you.

If any of this sounds familiar, this book is the right read for you at this point in your life. How lucky are we that this familiar pain is mirrored back at the very moment you need it? Now, I will take you through a journey to help you take your life back, one precious minute at a time, so you can kick ass at work and life and everywhere you want.

CHAPTER 2
REVOLUTION

Sometimes, there's an event that triggers a path you didn't expect or couldn't prepare for. A revolution of sorts. In this chapter, I'll tell you the story of my own corporate path, the slow burn that led to eventual burnout, and the moment that changed everything and brought me to tears.

Years ago, I graduated college with a bachelor's degree in food science and found my way to a corporate research and development role at Mars, Incorporated. I was spending time doing what I thought was my calling, and yet I felt I wanted a different experience. I moved around to different roles until I landed in the human resources department, where I was responsible for talent management processes such as performance reviews, development planning, and succession planning. It was in this role that I got exposure to executive coaching, as we'd pair coaches with our leaders to help them grow professionally.

Executive coaches have a powerful presence and a tough-love way of holding up the mirror to their clients, to help them know what needs to shift in their professional world. They possess an ability to unlock a client's development goals, as well as those of their bosses, peers, or the whole team. As I watched the coaches and came to better understand their styles and impact, their actions and being resonated with me.

At the time, I had never received coaching, and I had never been in the role of coach. Yet I was intuitively drawn toward their presence and teachings. I longed for a broader and deeper understanding of myself. I longed for a connection with myself, tying together the person inside and outside of work. And, I longed to become a version of myself who achieved goals that *I wanted* — not the goals that I created as a result of a 360-feedback survey. Maybe you can relate to this longing for something more or different. Maybe you are looking for clarity about what it is or how to get there.

For me, I loved the idea of being a coach. I wanted to be the catalyst that turned on other people's lightbulbs or helped them to shine more brightly. It was a seed planted deep within, a "someday, maybe" thought stored away in the potting shed until a future spring-cleaning of the greenhouse. As I mentioned, I didn't know what to do with this intuition just yet, so there the seed lay dormant until a future calling would provide the nutrients needed.

I moved on once again to a new HR role, in which I was the generalist at a startup company within the corporation. All of the tools and processes I helped develop over time as a human resource specialist were now mine to implement in the business as a generalist. It gave me great empathy to be on the other side of the equation — to own the implementation of the process instead of the theory of it. While it was a great growth experience for me professionally, I was also going through personal growth — on the inside. You see, I was finally pregnant after many natural and intervention-method attempts. Since I was in the early stages of an IVF pregnancy, I wasn't sure if I had one or two babies on the rise. I remember it being a very stressful time for my husband, Nick, and me, yet very exciting, as we embarked on growing our family beyond the two of us.

Hormones and uncertainty aside, nothing slowed down on the work front. In fact, being part of a startup within an established corporation had many pioneering challenges that went beyond what a typical workday might be for someone who works within a well-oiled machine. I found it hard to balance self-care of progesterone shots, frequent doctor visits, lack of sleep, and the growing pains that go along with building a new life on the inside while I was building a new organization in my work world. (I'm sure you have had this thought or a similar one before: "Will work ever be slow enough for me to focus on the rest of my life?")

After a successful pregnancy, we gave birth to our first child, a girl named Olivia. We were thrilled to have made it so far and to have a healthy life join the Full party! Since my husband and I share the same values, we thought it was important for Olivia to have a parent at home who would be around to raise her as much as possible. My husband and I, both corporate warriors at the same parent corporation, very much took pride in our work and career paths. Since my pioneering position was more demanding than his at the time, we decided he would take a career break and work part time, while I stayed full time. Even now, my husband will say that this break, to raise a child, was one of the highpoints of his lifetime.

With that decision made, I continued to work all the hours and all the days, hauling my breast pump to work where I'd hold a picture of Olivia during pump time, believing I was doing the best I could for her and my family. Perhaps this sounds familiar to parents out there: It was definitely a happy time, but it was also the most tiring time in my life.

A typical day in my workweek would involve waking from one of the two-hour clips of sleep I'd get after having nursed all night with a co-sleeping babe. The alarm would indicate the final end of the sleep-attempt slugs. Then, I would start an early morning with a super quick shower with Olivia in the bouncy chair or in the co-sleeper, if it was a day Nick was off. I'd do my final prep of lunch packing, breast pump bag and supplies, and last good-byes to my little and husband — or nanny, if it was a career day for both of us — and head off on my 45-minute commute.

During the commute, I'd take calls or amp myself up with my favorite tunes and transition from mom to leadership team member. From the moment I was at work, I'd be engaged with the associates, my boss, peers, and my laptop pretty much nonstop until nature called in some fashion. I bet you know that drill! And it was equally important to me to keep my nutrition, hydration, and milk supply high while I was committed to keeping engagement and productivity high at work. I'd take breaks to pump, and I'd call home to see how Olivia was holding up. I'd like to be able to report that it was seamless, but Olivia had other plans.

My daughter was the baby whom no one could hold or feed easily except me. Everyone thought I was overprotective or neurotic when I'd say, "No thank you, she'll scream her face off," when others wanted to hold her.

"Nonsense!" they'd say, "I'm the baby whisperer, give me that child."

But Olivia would scream and cry like it was her job. And, let's face it, it was — babies are so in tune with what they want that anything other than it results in a fit. How great of a tool is *that*? And how unfortunate is it that our connection to our needs seems to get beat out of us as we age? We'll get into that a bit later in the book.

On these calls home, I'd ask how it was going. Often, Olivia would not take a bottle of mom's milk — not all day long. You can imagine how "fun" it was for anyone who was watching her — and extra fun for me once I walked in the door. If it was an especially tough day, I'd try to leave work a bit early to give Olivia, Nick or the childcare provider, myself, and my boobs some relief.

Sometimes, it didn't work out that way, and I wouldn't have time to pump again. After the long workday and longish commute, I was like an extra-full water cooler during the playoff game the second I walked in the door and that baby cried. "Hike!" was shouted. Immediate football hand-off, work jersey ripped off, scrambling, ravenous, nipple-seeking child heading straight for the goal line. "Touchdown!" the crowd cheers. After all, the excitement, there is a lull for the drunken, milk-fed mini-athlete, and all the coaches exhale and relax.

The nighttime routine (and I mean the hours between 6 p.m. and 10 p.m.) was filled with chores, meal prep and consumption, and bath time and bedtime routines. Although, who are we kidding? There won't be any real sleep happening that night. While still connected to my email, I'd be catching up on the work world so that I didn't walk into a storm the next day. And the co-sleeping began, a combination of nursing and REM-failed attempts.

There's the alarm again! Already? And away we go....

Fast-forward to IVF pregnancy number two, about 18 months later. I'm still working full time while breast-feeding a toddler, and I'm starting to consider the next phase of my career. I was in love with my growing family, but I wasn't in love with my work. The role of human resources (God bless every person who works in it) felt more like that of a rule enforcer to me than anything else. Now, if any of you happen to work in that role, hold off on the judgment for a minute. I know full well there are plenty of talented, capable, HR catalysts out there, each of whom sees and handles this role very differently. I was in a place where I did not love the structure. It felt like I was holding myself and others back with my approach and skill set. I was longing for a role that allowed more freedom and flexibility, more possibilities and potential. It was beyond a longing, if I'm honest. I felt trapped by my circumstances. Not that anyone was trapping me — I just didn't know how to unwind my perspective enough to be different in this role or to unlock my own potential moving forward.

Thank God I had the awareness and the vulnerability to realize I couldn't figure out my next step on my own. At first, I felt like I didn't have the clarity to know how to map out the next part of my life, not even my next immediate step. Then, I remembered my little, dormant seed. I sought out a life coach to help me get a handle on my path, as well as to understand what it would take to *be* a coach for others. With my own money, I hired Stephanie Yost, my first life coach, and started the process of figuring out my life, both personally and professionally.

Through this process, I became aware that I wanted to be a coach like the person who was helping me to get clear and transform. I signed up with the Coaches Training Institute (CTI) and, while still working full time, began learning the fundamentals and doing the coursework required for me to become a coach. Rather than trying to help a client fix a specific aspect of their life, such as their work performance, life coaches help their clients to look at the big picture, evaluating their lives holistically and making changes. It was during this coach training that I had a breakthrough (or breakdown?) that changed everything for me.

In order to keep up with the fast pace and high workload of my job, I often went to coach training on weekends, where I traveled far enough from home to need a hotel. I also had to bring childcare with me for the toddler I was still nursing while being very pregnant building baby number two. Like you, I was trying to do it all and do it all well. I didn't miss a beat at work and that was at the expense of any sleep let alone fun in my downtime. I wanted to be a present mom, a good wife, a dedicated employee, and a growing human — both personally and professionally. And I was incredibly exhausted and overwhelmed trying to meet everyone's needs.

During one of my coaching trainings, we were engaging in a Future Self visualization, in which I was shown my life twenty years in the future. I had a vision of a classic yellow school bus pulling away with my waving children in it saying, "Bye, mom!" In this vision, they were gone. Even though it was a "memory" of school-aged children in my vision, their departure in that bus symbolized that I had missed it all. Twenty years had gone by, and I was an empty nester. The tears burned through my tight eyelids as I sobbed that it was all over already, as if even this new life growing inside me had left the nest. I had never yet seen his or her face, and already the empty ache of loss and grief filled me instantaneously.

I knew right then and there that my lifestyle had to shift. The working all the time, without enough time for my family and myself... it had to stop immediately.

Intellectually, I knew I had been moving in that direction for some time — but I also knew someone had to pay the bills and provide for my family. My husband and I agreed to swap roles. He would go full time, and I would go part time while focusing on my coaching career and switching into mother-bear mode. This was still a hard choice for me, and the ego part that built a career as breadwinner and corporate pioneer of a budding business felt let down. You, too, may feel the sense of pride the ego serves up about all you've accomplished up to this point. Yet, it was a choice I made — or, I should say, it felt as if it was already made for me in that moment when I looked twenty years ahead.

This shift was the end of something, and the beginning of something bigger. I finished my coach training and moved on to get a full coach certification around the time I gave birth to our second-born, a baby boy named Raymond. During my maternity leave with Ray, I tried to develop a coach role inside the company where I worked to honor my passion while also serving the organization in a new capacity. But it didn't work out: It was an idea before its time, and the company truly needed a dedicated HR person who loved that role more than I did.

With a heavy and grateful heart, I gave my notice and left my corporate job. I ran toward a dream that I hadn't fully vetted yet. I had no real business plan or waitlist of clients. Yes, I had my husband's support — and pay and benefits — but I was used to being the breadwinner, and we needed my salary to live. (Perhaps you have similar fears about risking the money, the benefits, the ability to pay the mortgage while still being a heavy hitter in this game of life.) It was incredibly scary to make this jump with no guarantee of the corporate parachute. But I had clarity about what I wanted; I was reminded of a quote from the movie *When Harry Met Sally*: "I knew. I knew the way you know about a good melon."

Within two weeks of leaving, I landed my first client and never looked back. My business has been growing and thriving since 2010 through word of mouth and referrals. Over one and a half years, as well as a year of coach training, I worked with my own coach to get clear on what I needed to do and who I needed to *be* in order to serve in this capacity. The gravitational pull of possibility became too strong to live any other way.

Am I saying you need to leave your job to be happy? Hell no — quite the opposite. I'm saying that my path led me this way. I left my corporate job to follow my life's purpose so that you don't necessarily have to leave your job to live yours.

Let me be clear: This is not a late night, insomnia-driven informercial that states, "You too can be just as fulfilled as I am with never a worry again!" My struggles and growth are not over. My ego still comes into play and I am far from living the perfect life with perfect choices. I do the work I'm inviting you to do. I'm never without a coach in my life, as I truly need and desire someone who can hold a mirror to my world, and who helps me get out of my own story. And yet I have coached hundreds of clients over the last decade and have learned the frequent offenses and best-applied tactics to help you make the shifts you are seeking ASAP. Take heed and know that you'll get results and relief along with the resilience to keep at it when the fairy tale isn't going as you thought it would.

There are endless choices you can make to be more fulfilled. We will explore with confidence how yours will evolve in the next chapter.

CHAPTER 3
EVOLUTION

As we read, my story involved a leap of faith outside my corporate comfort zone. However, not all scenarios involve such a drastic shift in order to claim back your life.

Meet one of my clients, a married mom of one and a corporate VP who we will call Rachel. Rachel was struggling with finding time to exercise in the midst of a busy workweek. She was feeling guilty if she got up early to run or if she ran after work because both of those options meant taking time away from her family. Plus, it was the darkest time of year, and she didn't feel safe running outside near the office during the bookend parts of the day. By waiting to do weekend-warrior mileage, she wasn't getting the benefits of the endorphin release that she desperately needed daily. The thought of running during work hours was blasphemy. I mean, what would her boss say? What would her team think? Rachel felt like a slacker either way, as both a leader and as an athlete, because this piece of her was missing.

After coaching about this, she decided she was going to run during her lunch break for a mile or two, just to see how she felt and what consequences she had to manage upon her return. You know what terrible things happened? None. Not one bad consequence for running during her lunch break. Everyone who witnessed it either accepted it or was motivated by it because she was a role model for making a decision to be a better, holistic human, which also made her a better leader at work. Each situation will be different, but without taking a chance, you'll never know what's possible.

Imagine a version of your life in which there is enough time to balance it all in a way you love. You have a career that's rewarding and fulfilling. There's time for family and fun and yourself — the elusive "me time" that we read about only in *Oprah* and *Self* magazines. You find yourself feeling fine whether it's Monday morning or Friday night — it's just the same because you are striking a balance that feeds all parts of you. Think this is a colossal joke? I invite you to reconsider.

I've coached hundreds of corporate warriors who are so dedicated to work that they forget about themselves in the process. I often remind them of the wonderful value that they provide in being such dedicated workers and leaders. I also remind them that they are doing the best they can with current tools and states of mind. And yet, the invitation to *be* better vs. *do* better is always there, waiting for the aware, the willing, and the able.

It goes a little something like this: Too often everyone else gets the best of you. You are happy and proud to give of yourself to your career and to whoever needs you. Until you burn out. But what about *you* needing you? Aren't you worth it too?

Imagine this: you get to be the client of your own awesomeness.

There is a world in which, when you win, everyone wins. And it's not another deadline, job, or lifetime away. It's closer than you think. Typically, there are a lot of doubts and fears that rear their ugly heads when I speak of such tomfoolery as "work life balance."

I've heard it all, and maybe some of these thoughts, often expressed by my clients, resonate with you:

- "I can't sleep well at night because I can't shut my brain off from the never-ending list."
- "Because I work so much, I feel guilty taking time for me after work when my family is waiting."
- "I don't have time to work out."
- "There aren't enough hours in the day to get it all done."
- "I'm afraid I'll regret not being there for my kids' important milestones."
- "If I don't answer every email, I get anxious I'll miss something."
- "I'm a go-getter and people count on me, so 'me time' isn't an option."
- "It feels so selfish to get my nails done when I should be helping at home."
- "If I say no to tasks or to people, I won't be viewed as a team player."
- "If I delegate, then it won't get done right or on time. It's easier for me to do it myself."

If any or all of these lines sound familiar, or you'd like to insert your own personal hell statement, please know that you are not alone. You are a normal corporate warrior working on autopilot at the moment.

Whether you have a revelation like I did that shakes you awake, or you are in a state of slower evolution, just know it's quite common to be uncomfortable with big change. You may even feel that, by putting yourself first, you're being selfish. So many years of conditioning have led you to believe that this is the truth. I'd like to invite you to think of it as being self-serving — but not selfish. You've likely heard the quote by author Eleanor Brown, who said, "You cannot pour from an empty vessel." Unless you have a magic trick that I don't know about, I'm sure this is true for you as well.

Lots of feelings or fears may come up when you consider making any changes in your life right now. After all, you have a great job with pay and benefits, and perhaps a lot of things are going really well in your life. But, given that, why not make it even better? Why not allow it to be even easier? Why not dream a bit and see what's possible for you?

This book is going to take you on a journey. You'll face whatever your current state is and move through steps to help you create the balanced life you love, both at work and home. The steps and tools provided in this book come from the practices I employ with my clients on a daily basis in order to move from overwhelm and stress towards peace and confidence.

In the next chapter, Chapter Four, we will explore the first step: *awareness*. We will look at how you are feeling and what you are doing right now with curiosity. If you are going to go on a journey, you have to know where to find your starting point. If, after achieving this awareness, you choose to do nothing, that's okay! It's just the first step toward any progress, and odds are you'll want more for yourself than what you have.

In Chapter Five, we will move toward *acceptance* of your awareness with zero judgment. While you are still not creating major external change in your life, the shifts are starting internally. You have more choice than you realize when it comes to attitude and perspective, even if you feel conflicted about acting on it just yet.

Chapter Six will cover one of the best navigational tools in your toolkit: your *values*. Your values are a set of beliefs that are critically important and non-negotiable for you. In this chapter, you will explore the belief systems that get in the way of living fully and unapologetically, and you will know how to use your values and beliefs as your compass for powerful choice.

In Chapter Seven, I'll ask you the question, "Who's the boss of you, anyway?" Wondering what the answer is? Well, obviously *you*! In this chapter, you will learn and apply tools to shift your inner game, inspire your outer game actions, and create structures and boundaries for self-care.

Then, in Chapter Eight, you are invited to trust your Higher Power, however you define that. Think of it like how you trust the navigation system in your car when you can't see how it operates. You will learn tools that help you get clear on your guidance.

In Chapter Nine, you will build off the foundation of short-term actions by painting your future vision and exploring your best life possible.

In Chapter Ten, you'll be encouraged to move past obstacles and be grounded in traditional leadership skills, which will help all of the internal work you've done up to this point. You will see how this all comes to life in your relationships at work and at home.

Finally, in Chapter Eleven, you will synthesize all of the lessons from the book, so that you will understand that we don't arrive anywhere on this journey. Rather, we continue the cycle of *Thriveability* and learn more options to amp up our lives for sustainable change.

I'm so happy you are here! Let's find out where here is — in the next chapter.

CHAPTER 4
YOU ARE HERE

Before I take on a new client, I ask them the following question about their life: "On a scale of 1 to 10, how much pain are you in?" One means the pain is barely there; ten is the worst pain ever. It's as if we are in the emergency room of life when the doctor asks you to choose the emoji face corresponding to your pain level. While I'm using the word pain, it's really referring to stress and how well you are tolerating it. If the client answers with anything below an eight, I question whether we need to work together just yet. We can go a long time in tolerate mode, and I often find that, unless things are super painful, there isn't much of a hunger to shift anything about your life. Granted, there are always exceptions, but a client's pain level is the first indication to me of their awareness about their life.

If we know the pain (the level, the triggers, etc.), then we can eventually do something about it. Without awareness of the pain, it's as if a phantom put a "kick me" sign on our back, leaving us to wonder why we are beat up.

Achieving this awareness is key. It helps you understands what is going on presently in order to make choices moving forward. It is being wide awake about current state in order to shape future state. What we will not do is ask the "why" questions of the past. Why do I have this pattern? Why did I make that choice? Etc. I am not trained appropriately to help you look in the rearview mirror and psychoanalyze your past and why you are the way you are.

Therapy, counseling, and other methods are great options to collect that intel and even heal. What coaching does is address the present state and help you look forward through the windshield to navigate and choose powerfully.

In this chapter, we will explore your awareness before moving forward. "No pain, no gain," the saying goes — but this is about "know pain, know gain." You'll need to gain that knowledge through increasing your awareness mentally and physically before moving on to action. We will also look at how you are feeling and what you are currently doing about it. By the end of this chapter, you will be wide awake about the triggers in your work and in your life — and may be poised to take further action.

Achieving Awareness

If you are reading this book and looking for relief, evaluating your pain is a good place to start. There is no need to do anything yet with this information; first, we just want to be aware of what's going on in this snapshot in time, knowing that tomorrow or last week it could be different.

To facilitate this awareness, take a moment to put your hand on your heart, take a deep breath in and out, and answer the following question: "On a scale from 1 to 10, how much pain am I in?"

Check in and let a number come to you. Write it down. Now, pay attention to where you are physically feeling this pain. It could be a tightness in your jaw, tenseness in your shoulders, a bit of nausea in your stomach. Or, maybe you have a hard time with this and feel a headache because you are overthinking the exercise. There is no right or wrong answer, only awareness of what's going on.

The reason the physical connection is so important is because our body is our best truth meter. It senses that something is wrong long before we know there is a "kick me" sign. I'm sure you have discovered your own evidence of this. Maybe your immune system crashes just in time for that vacation you planned. Or, maybe your skin breaks out in a rash. Maybe you have unexplained back pain, a headache or acid reflux visits you because you are holding your stress in your stomach. Everyone will have their version of the evidence, and yours might show up differently, depending on the issue, the pain level, or the circumstances.

Continuing with the exercise, we have a number and we have a physical cue to match it. Let's assume for this exercise that you are at a 10 out of 10: You are completely fed up with your work life balance being out of whack, and you can't imagine another week at this pace. You check in with your body. Complete the following sentence: "I feel this pain/stress in my _____."

The only thing to do at this point is notice it. Acknowledge it. Be with it. There is no need to stretch away the kink or try to outrun it. Just notice it and write it down if you want to check for future patterns. This habit of noticing the discord and the related physical clue will help you manage in reverse eventually.

Let's take the case of Christi, for example. She's in a meeting, and once again the topic of the campaign comes up. They want a redo. She's worked hard at this, and the prospect of more churn feels like the product of others' poor decision making. She's frustrated even though she hasn't connected the dots yet to explore how she's feeling; she's still keeping her game face on in front of the dozen colleagues around the table. But her façade isn't telling the truth. She might even believe she's keeping her cool in the meeting, but her body is saying otherwise. Her jaw tightens and she's white knuckling her pen as she tries to stay engaged in the conversation.

Later, if Christi is aware of her body cues, she can work backwards to identify the trigger in the meeting and better understand how she felt about it in the moment. The body doesn't lie. This is all part of the awareness game.

Fighting Overwhelm

You know this ten that you are at right now, and you feel it in your bones. You may have even called it "overwhelm." I know I've felt overwhelm, this feeling of "there's just too much to do, not enough time, and in no way am I going to meet the expectations of others let alone myself any time soon." Overwhelm will manifest in your body the same way any of the other triggers will. Maybe it's shortness of breath, like a mini panic attack. Or, perhaps your sleep is affected, since your brain won't shut down with all the to-do list items. Now, your body is sending you the "truth" that something is wrong, but overwhelm is a liar, a trickster.

Overwhelm creates problems that don't exist yet, similar to its cousin, Worry. My dad has this quote of William Ralph Inge, "Worry is interest paid on trouble before it comes due." While it feels oh so real in our world, overwhelm isn't really happening right this moment. It's usually a symptom of the projection of what's to come in the future (the big-ass to-do list), or perhaps it's the result of marinating in stuff gone wrong this week (in the past). It's not really happening in this nanosecond.

How do we squash overwhelm? One of the best ways to reel it in and to anchor yourself in the now is through conscious, purposeful breathing. We already breathe on autopilot (thank God for that). And to truly focus on our breathing is magic. All time slows down. This is not a new method by any means. For instance, practices of yoga, meditation, mindfulness, and even athletics all involve breathwork. When you are in a state of pain, the key is to recognize that state and remember that overwhelm has you spinning anywhere but *here*, where you need to be. Breath is the path back to your present moment.

There is a tactic called breath awareness, in which you are not attempting to control your breathing at all, but rather to just notice its pace without judgment or agenda. Somehow, for me, I tend to slow down and focus automatically when practicing breath awareness. You can try and see how this works for you.

One of my favorite methods of controlled breathing is called *square breathing,* or the four-part breath. You breathe in for four seconds, hold it for four seconds, exhale for four seconds, and hold it for four seconds. Repeat. You can do this in the middle of a meeting or during a road rage episode when you want to scream or lose it. No one needs to know what you are doing to stay grounded. You are breathing anyway! It's free, it's immediate, and it's almost invisible.

A tactic I use to stay focused during square breathing in a meeting setting is to doodle the square as I count to myself. The first side of the square takes me four seconds to draw. Then, the second, third, and fourth sides all each take four seconds. Next, I trace around the square as I keep breathing for a few cycles. It's quite relaxing and brings me to the present moment because I have to focus on the counting, the drawing, and the breathing. There is no room for overwhelm in this moment; no room for worrying that I didn't defrost meat for dinner or that the to-do list keeps growing because I'm in too many meetings.

This moment of peace, albeit fleeting at times, is so helpful to get clear on what the triggers are that set you off. When you feel life is driving you (and you aren't driving life), a little sanity in the moment can help you see the road clearly.

Know Your Values

I've mentioned triggers a few times. They are any moment that kicks us off our A-game. We all have them, and I'd be lying if I said the goal in life is to never be triggered. Sometimes I wish I was totally Zen, but how would I know what's truly important to me if I'm not set off from time to time? Through the looking glass of these triggers we can see what's important to us at our core: *our values*. During coach training at CTI, we spent much time defining who we are at our core. We do not choose our values, and they are not morals or principles; rather, they are intrinsically *us*.

Let's look at an example at work. You have a team member who is always late. You've learned to expect this from them, but you are still fuming when they show up with their litany of excuses ten minutes past the hour. Which of your values is being challenged here? Punctuality? Respect? Productivity? It could be any number of values. A need you have is being unmet, and you have a reaction.

In comes the pain — ask yourself how severe it is and where it's showing up in your body. And, if needed, you can breathe through it to get clear on what the value is that just got stepped on.

Notice that you still didn't act differently yet, even if you have accomplished breathing in a more focused way. You are still just being aware of what's going on. We will discuss values more deeply in Chapter 6 and how to use them as a compass of sorts. For now, we just want to walk around wide awake about them, even if we don't do anything differently.

For a moment, let's consider if your pain number was at a five. I mentioned earlier that this number would likely indicate that you are not yet ready to do much differently; you are in tolerate mode. Even tolerating gives us data and reveals our values. It's important to ask yourself what you are tolerating and follow up with a question about trade-offs. For example, if you are tolerating a colleague being late each time you meet, and you are not truly triggered to a ten, then what are you choosing instead? Perhaps you like to keep the peace, so you are choosing that over addressing the tardiness. If you tend to just move on with old habits, you may have never looked closely at your patterns and identified what's important to you.

How does all this awareness relate to time management and work life balance? Well, you cannot fix what you are not aware of. You wouldn't do this at work would you? Just start trying to solve for things without a foundation of what you already know? The pain scale helps us prioritize. It helps us know whether a problem is something worth addressing ASAP, or whether we can continue to tolerate it in service of something else that's more important to us at the moment.

The awareness I discussed up to this point is mostly reactive. Let's recap. You are in pain, and you are looking closely at where in your body it's showing up. The pain was triggered by something, and now you are searching for the value it might be butting up against. Then next tool you will use is an *assessment* of your whole life, so that you can be holistically aware of yourself and your pain level.

The Wheel of Life

I always send a copy of the "Wheel of Life" in my new client packet. The "Wheel of Life" provides a method for capturing a snapshot in time showing how fulfilled we are in several key areas. You may have seen versions of this wheel before, or it may be a brand-new concept. Even if you are a veteran of this process, it's always good to see where you are today and reset, since fulfillment changes frequently.

I have amended the traditional version of the wheel based on my years of experience with clients and the categories we coach most frequently. My latest version has twelve categories:

- Career
- Money
- Health
- Romance/Significant Other
- Fun and Recreation
- Family
- Friends
- Support System
- Personal Development

- Physical Environment
- Self-care
- Higher Power/Higher Self

To create the wheel, draw a circle and divide it into 12 slices like you are cutting a pizza pie. Label each slice on the perimeter of the wheel with one of the categories above until each slice is labeled. For a downloadable worksheet of the Live Full Coaching version of the Wheel of Life, please see the resource section of my website: (http://www.livefullcoaching.com/book-buyers/).

When you consider these categories, you are looking to assess where you are in each one on a fulfillment scale of 0 to 10, 0 being the lowest, 10 being the highest. Remember, this is not a quantity game, but a quality game. It's the relationship with the category that is important. For example, let's look at money. There are plenty of people who, by societal standards, are on the higher end of the income spectrum, yet live in fear about money and feel they never have enough. They would give a low rating to that category. There are just as many people who live within their means and have a healthy relationship with money. They may make way less than their fearful peers, and yet they can still rate that category very highly. This isn't a test you need to pass — it's part of awareness, allowing you to see the whole picture of your very dynamic life.

When you are ready to do the assessment, try not to overthink it. Just fill in a number rather quickly based on your first reaction to each category. At first pass, you may notice some guilt or resistance showing up. Don't let the "shoulds" hit the fan. Resist thinking, "I should work out more," or, "I should save more money"; try to block out all of the other similar should-a, could-a, would-a statements that aren't really helpful. Set them aside and look at what your fulfillment meter is actually telling you.

Remember, too, that if you rate something a ten, it doesn't mean you don't have any goals left with this category. I coach many perfectionists, who remind me and themselves that they never give anything 10 out of 10 because there is always room for improvement. They say, "I'll give it a 9.5." Yes, I get that. But you aren't robbing yourself of anything either if it's honestly a ten! If you feel genuinely fulfilled in a category, give it the ten. I promise that it's not likely to stay there for long because, as your perspective shifts, so does your assessment.

Here is a summary of what each category means and the intention of rating it:

Career. You may have a role you love and that is fulfilling, even though you work seventy hours a week. If it's your dream job, and you are truly fulfilled, then rate it with a high number. Conversely, you may have a title and power, but your job still doesn't speak to your soul. In that case, rate it accordingly.

Money. Like it or not, we live in a world where this is a necessity. How you feel about what you do with your money (earning it, saving it, spending it, donating it, lending it, etc.) all impacts the mojo around it. On a scale of 1 to 10, how fulfilled are you by your relationship with money? One of my favorite exercises to do involves asking the question, "If money was your lover, how are you treating them?" Are you trusting with money, or are you hitting refresh on your bank account every hour to see if it "came home" yet? Do you have a lot of rules around it that cause anxiety? Think about money as if it were a person, how do you think money would react to your vibe? Rate this category in terms of fulfillment within that relationship, not in terms of quantity.

Health. Again, I realize this could always be better and that you may have some very personal challenges or goals. Still, you want to take the snapshot of today and assess what your fulfillment is in relation to your health. Another example: there could be a body builder with 3 percent body fat who is still super upset about their hereditary high cholesterol problem. Compare that to a 70-year-old who isn't winning any contests but is happy to be alive, walking around on their own power, and is cancer-free. Yahtzee!

Romance/Significant Other. You may be happily married or happily divorced. You may be single and feel lonely. Or, you may be single and loving it. There is no perfect scenario here; just look at how fulfilled you are within this category. And, I must share that one time (and one time only) I was asked the question, "What if romance is separate from significant other?" Well, then I suppose you can rate them separately, no judgment here.

Fun and Recreation. Yes, it's a thing! That fun you say you need to create more time for in the future — let's rate where your fulfillment stands right now. You may find that the once-per-year, rent-an-island splurge just isn't enough. You'd feel more fulfilled with daily laughs at this point to break up the burnout. Whatever it is, we aren't solution-finding yet – just assessing.

Family. This category, like the friends' category below, is all about quality of the relationship, not quantity. Consider your immediate or extended family relationships and the people who are most important to you. How fulfilled are you with these relationships?

Friends. Think of this the same way you did the previous category. When I first rated this category, I rated it low because I focused on how few friends I had. And then I realized that I love and adore the few I have like family. Only then did I realize that this wasn't a quantity game at all! Your rating should be based on the fulfillment you get from the friendships you have. You may find you have some toxic relationships too in these categories that lead you feeling drained. Your fulfillment rating will reflect this as well.

Support System. I added this category because I realized how important it is to receive just as much as it is to give. Who are your champions and support system in your busy life? This includes physical support like childcare or housecleaning, and emotional/mental support, such as a life coach, mentor, group leader, or therapist. From a leadership perspective, who supports you at work? Rate how fulfilled you are with your current support system.

Personal Development. It is important that you assess this category from a perspective that is not strictly related to professional development. How are you developing your talents, interests, or hobbies? What is stretching your mind, body, and spirit beyond work training? Rate the fulfillment you currently get from this category.

Physical Environment. This can be the most ambiguous of the categories. Think of where you physically spend most of your time, whether it's your open office environment, a less-than-ideal-work-from-home set up, a house that needs a ton of repairs, a car your love (or can't stand) when you travel. The level of fulfillment you get from where you are physically depends on how your surroundings are impacting your energy and mood. I'll share a brief, personal example.

When I first left my corporate job, I had a newborn and a two-year-old at home with a nanny while I was building my own business. I had one nursery to the right of my office, the other bedroom to the left, and I couldn't coach on the phone because the children would hear me and have meltdowns. I found myself leaving and coaching in my car just to have some sacred space to change the lives of my clients. I was considering renting space above a local Starbucks. My physical environment rating was in the tank! Yes, I had a safe, nice home, but the impact it had on my business was such a drag that I wanted to move. We soon found a home with a detached office, and I am now at a bursting 10 out of 10 with my physical environment. I hope this example helps you rate your physical environment score when considering your own situation.

Self-care. Oh yes, this is its own category. I added this to the wheel to ensure focus and to elevate its importance — however you define "self-care" or "me time." You may find that there is some overlap, but this is true for any and all of the categories. Self-care may mean massages, meditation, exercise, avoiding drama and gossip, or hiding away in the bathroom reading a fiction novel in peace for ten minutes. Please rate how fulfilled you are in this category based on what you consider self-care to be for you.

Higher Power/Higher Self. This category relates to however you define that which is greater than you. Whether you believe in God, Christ, Source, Buddha, Mother Nature, the Universe, overall energy and Law of Attraction or your best, highest self, it is something bigger than just you, grunting it out on this planet. How is your relationship with this category? Let's say you don't believe in anything at all, but you are 100 percent at peace with that. In that case, you may want to give it a higher ranking because you feel grounded.

Once you've rated each category, date the paper and just look at the whole picture. Where are the strengths? Where are the opportunities? Remember the guidelines we've addressed:

- Quality and relationship, not quantity.
- Don't overthink it.
- A ten doesn't mean you don't have goals anymore.
- Watch for the should-, could-, would-haves (an indication that your inner critic may have been the one rating this time around).

We are still in awareness, people! Still no is action necessary. You can, if you so choose, make the paper on which you rated each category into an origami bird and fly it out the window. I just want you to look for emerging themes, surprises, and validation. How did it feel to fill it out? Often, people get sad, perhaps due to a recent loss in their life, or perhaps because they just ripped off the blindfold to reveal their world perspective. My corporate clients' first reaction is that they can't believe career is just one pie slice because they spend so much time either at work or thinking about work. And, there it is, folks — the reality that you are a dynamic, multi-faceted human, with much to give and receive beyond work.

All of these categories can impact each other. One can raise others like the tide that lifts all boats. If you gave "money" a high rating, for example, perhaps you can throw money at other areas in which you are less fulfilled, such as "fun" or "support systems." Conversely, a low fulfillment score can sink others, like when an inflatable pool float gets a tear when six kids jump on it. It is important to acknowledge what's working well, just as much as it's important to acknowledge what's weighing you down. So much good can happen when you leverage your strengths. Just notice your own assessment of this snapshot in time and try to be kind to yourself.

As a recap, we have done a lot in this first step. Awareness takes courage, honesty, and vulnerability to even see the "kick me" sign, let alone start to remove it. You've learned how awareness impacts your body and physicality; how breathing helps us be in the moment and provide some clarity about the now. Things that are important to you, such as your values, trigger you. You've seen how dynamic your life is. All of these elements are like looking at the faceted fun-house mirror of your life for data in order to move forward. Now that you know pain, you can know gain. In this next chapter, we will explore what's next for you — now that you are an awareness machine.

CHAPTER 5
THE PATH TO POWERFUL CHOICES

You just learned how to walk, wide awake, around your world. Now that you can see where you're going, you can make better choices, right?! Yes, but not just yet. If we jumped into all kinds of action right now, it may lead to some shifts, but you first need to slow down in order to go faster.

I realize that this is counterintuitive to your "get 'er done" personality. In fact, I see most clients feel tasered by their own assessment on the Wheel of Life — so much so that they are jolted into a Nike commercial and just start doing it. Moving so quickly may get results. In fact, you will get results. However, if you want more sustainable results that are in full alignment with who you truly are, you need to consider a few things prior to taking action.

In this chapter, you will be taking that awareness from earlier and will move toward acceptance. Think of acceptance as ownership. You can be aware of something like an emotion but not really be mindful and own it. After we accept what is, then we can make choices about attitude before taking an external action. Once your attitude, or inner game, is aligned, it will translate to your actions, or outer game.

My clients hear me say, "powerful choice," quite frequently. For me, the term doesn't always mean some grand gesture, but it does mean that you are fully behind what you are deciding. It means that you own it 100 percent. You're full-assing it, so to speak, versus half-assing it. This could show up as something as simple as leaving work on time, even though an internal client did a drive by and asked if you *have a minute*. Normally, you'd say, "Sure, I have a minute, take a seat." However, we all know it's never just a minute. And while you want to serve and be there when needed, you are a bit more awake now about how you feel when you give away all of these minutes.

So, you make a powerful choice and say, "You matter, and so does this topic. And you deserve my full attention. When can we schedule a conversation at a time that meets both of our needs?" Sounds impossible, right? Well, it's fully possible, so let's explore what needs to happen in order to do this with integrity and a smile.

Reaching Acceptance

This chapter is all about the guts. Powerful choice is an inside job. By using our awareness and "body feels" as data, we can now explore the impact of our choices. There's one more step before we act from awareness, and that's *acceptance*. Acceptance doesn't mean we've settled or that we are at a standstill. It just means we are taking a level of honest ownership of what is here in the moment. I bet you've heard the abbreviated saying by Carl Jung, "What we resist, persists." That which we avoid tends to grow or get louder. And, if we are in denial about anything, it sure will bite us in the ass until we address the real deal.

There is some cleaning up that needs to be done here — a little internal housekeeping to make sure we aren't laying down this nice new rug of powerful choice on dirt and dust bunnies. Remember, as your coach, I'm not here to fix you or your past; it's not that kind of clean up. As your coach, I encounter you as naturally creative, resourceful, and whole (that's a CTI cornerstone), which means that you are not broken, and you do not need to be fixed. We are all spring boarding from a solid place. However, the internal energy or funk that may be swirling around us should be considered. We have reached a place where decisions are made, so let's be sure that place is as pure as possible. From great energy comes a great choice.

Let's take as an example one of the frequent-flyer triggers we explored earlier. You can know that you are addicted to nicotine. You are reminded about it when you feel a craving for that smokey treat, so there is no denial here. But, without accepting your addiction, you cannot move forward with a commitment to quit, go buy the patch, and see it through.

Another example: During the workday, you know you are double-booked. It's obvious because your calendar is a painful reminder of the layer-cake of meetings that can never all be tended to with your full attention. As long as you are in it-is-what-it-is mode, you won't be carving out white space anytime soon.

Where do we go from here? Start with something that you are motivated and excited to address, not something that comes from a place of obligation. Maybe the unhealthy habit of nicotine just feels too hard and sad to confront. Then let's not pick that first. Look for some low-hanging fruit that you will feel good to have accomplished — perhaps that means decluttering your schedule. Whatever problem you choose to address, it will give you energy to do it and have it done. Before we act, there's room for some inner-game work with our egos.

I judge myself harshly at times. I teach and coach about this, and yet, because I'm human, I still fall into the ego trap. I can be sad or get down about missing a goal, an injury that prevents me from excelling at sport or snapping at my kids because my expectations are so high. None of this feels good to me, and when that knee-jerk reaction or off-feeling creeps up, I feel like a failure.

In these cases, I'm the one who suffers most from uncontrolled emotion or self-deprecating behavior that doesn't serve anyone. My ego got in the way. I felt justified or right, and darn it, somebody's gonna pay! But often (almost always), I'm actually the one who pays for it. I recently learned from one of my life coaches, Dana Williams, to look for places that need forgiveness. Forgiveness aids us in accepting whatever is going on. It brings peace to a place you might have skipped over on your way to action. When I have that moment when I lack self-control (snapping at my kids), I remember to slow it down with breath, to be aware of my triggers and what's happening, and to forgive myself for the human moment.

Forgiveness doesn't right the wrong, just like saying you're sorry for being late to a meeting doesn't make you on time. However, the grace paves the way toward accepting and choosing differently in the future. It's a choice to heal versus a choice to be right (again, thank you Dana!). The more we practice awareness and acceptance, the more likely we will be to ward off the outbursts and adjust before they even happen (#goals).

Every single thing on the Wheel of Life, whether you rate it a 0 or a 10, stems from inner game. Inner game is a term that many athletes use in their training prior to the gymnastics meet or the critical swing on the 18th hole. For them and for us, it means we get results based on where we focus — not based on what we want.

I'll speak more to that idea later, but to simplify it now, I ask you to consider the truth at the core of the following idioms: you're in a foul mood because you "got up on the wrong side of the bed"; a chance meeting went awry because you "got off on the wrong foot." This practiced perspective is the lens through which we see the world or judge circumstances around us. Our starting mindset or mental story impacts the actions that follow. We are truly in charge of what happens next, so it is important to start with our attitudes. It is our powerful choice about the inner game that impacts our outer game.

After all of this awareness and acceptance, how do we shift our attitude? Grace leads the way to gratitude. Being truly grateful for what is working in our lives is the number one way to change your inner game from funk to fabulous. I have a real example to share about attitude and money.

I was working with a coach, Jeanna Gabellini, on my business vibe, model, and, of course, money. At the time, I was in a financial mudslide. Corporate payment terms were moving upwards of ninety days, and yet my bills were still weekly. I saw my savings tanking in an attempt to keep up with our expenses, and I started to freak out. I'm usually the one in our marriage who steeps in the abundance and trusting mindset, so when I worry, we all worry. Just as my financial well was drying up, the actual water well on our property dried up. No joke! The well was dry all around, and I couldn't help but engage in the laugh-cry-laugh cycle, as I shook my clenched fists at the humor of the Universe.

Remember the prompt earlier about money on the wheel? I asked you, "If money was your lover, how are you treating them?" Let me tell you, in the situation I was in, money stays the hell away from you! I was hitting refresh on my online bank account, chasing unpaid invoices, all with the constant feel of texting a potentially cheating partner, "Are you there yet? Where are you? When are you coming home?!"

Jeanna suggested I gratitude journal about anything and everything in my life, except money, in order to change the desperate vibe of my finances. For 30 days straight, I spent every morning writing in my gratitude journal about how grateful I was for the little and the big things in my life. A few examples follow:

- "I'm so grateful for my wood-burning insert and all of the cords of wood stacked outside my home. It keeps my house and family warm, and this makes me happy."
- "Thank you for my new Tahoe, this big safe vehicle that transports my three babes safely and gets me to my clients in the winter."
- "I'm so grateful I have my health and fitness. I'm able to get up every day, and work out, and feel good. I'm grateful for the health of my parents, husband, and children. We are all alive and healthy."

Just as I retype these words, I am filled with fulfillment. My breath is more meaningful, easier, and lighter. There is a tingle in my face, and I feel warm in my heart. Back then, this practice saved my life — not from my actual physical mortality, but from the mentality that was drying up my happiness, my finances, and, apparently, my real well.

Do you know that after those 30 days of gratitude journaling, the money came pouring in like a fire hydrant on a hot, summer day in the city? The great thing about gratitude is that you are appreciating what already is in the space. It's already here! So, there is no wanting or lacking or longing when we are grateful. It's pure appreciation, which then softens any resistance to receiving. Once I was able to fully appreciate what I already had, the money flowed easily.

Now, it took me 30 days in this example, but there is no perfect equation for this. Keep going with a gratitude attitude practice and notice what shifts for you. Try not to have an agenda. I know that's hard, but being tied to the outcome as a metric for success brings in more resistance.

Here is another way to look at it: focus on what you can control such as your thoughts. It's the difference between your intention vs. your expectation. Your intention is *internal*. How do you want to be? What is your emotional strategy to handle what's coming up? This is fully within your ability to guide and steer. What is common and crazymaking is trying to control the outcome. Expectation is *external*. You think, *if I do this, then I expect that*. It's a trap that causes much disappointment. Here are a few examples, and we'll start with the workplace.

Workplace Example:

Intention: "I'll host an associate appreciation party to show my team how much I value them. It will feel good to me just to follow through on this gesture, regardless of their reaction."

Expectation: "I'll host an associate appreciation party so that my team will be happy and appreciate me back. Their reaction will help with retention and engagement."

Personal Example:

Intention: "I'll invite my friends over for a gathering because it feels good to me to be inclusive. I love to give and share my time and love with them."

Expectation: "I'll invite my friends over for a gathering because they'll be so grateful, and we will have so much fun together. Then they will include me in their next gathering."

Notice how the inner game of intention is independent of the external reaction? The expectation is 100 percent tied to an external reaction you cannot control. I share this with you hoping you will find confidence and peace by focusing on what you can control and by letting go of the things you can't. The Serenity Prayer really nails it: "God, grant me the serenity to accept the things I cannot change, the courage to change the things I can, and the wisdom to know the difference." I often start my day by saying that prayer with my children before the day starts, especially during school, to help them understand the difference between intention and expectation.

Usually, any type-A personality has a beef with this type of exercise because they believe I'm asking them to give up complete control. Rejoice, control freaks! Me included. Become an inner-game mind-master, an intention ninja! That is the new game. And once again you can see we didn't even *do* anything differently yet. We are *being* differently.

Your Inner Critic

While staying within our inner-game circle, I'd like to shine the light into the shadows for a moment. It's a tall order to stay positive all the time and take refuge in the fact that we can control our thoughts.

I liken it to the thoughts that sweep in during meditation. You try to be all Zen-like, breathe, and close your eyes, then BAM! The to-do list starts like an old-school movie reel in your mind. The click-clack of the projector and the staticky soundtrack remind you not to forget to do all of the too-many-things you set out to do. You can't always control the thoughts that visit you, but you can process and redirect them, so that they don't camp out for long.

Let's play this out with a real inner critic voice that just loves to visit and sabotage your day. I learned this process through CTI, but there are many processes out there to help you manage your saboteur.

Imagine: You are sitting in a meeting, and you've just been given more responsibility for new a project when you are already overwhelmed with everything on your plate. Here comes the involuntary voice with a familiar message: "You aren't good enough to handle this." Yuck! And you believe this voice, too. Your face sort of scrunches up, and a sick feeling surfaces in your stomach. What do we do when we hear these less-than-supportive voices?

There are a few steps to follow. First, you want to write down the phrase or phrases this particular voice is fond of saying. Example: "You aren't good enough." Next, you want to personify the voice and give it mannerisms, a wardrobe, or a posture so that we can visualize this being when you hear its habitual chant. Then you name it! You can think of it as a younger version of you, or a parental figure, or a real person in your world — but you want to rename it so that it has its own identity. Make any tweaks to it so that you have a good sense of this being's presence when it visits.

Remember, there is a positive side to this shadow. Your inner critic is trying to serve you in some way or protect you from something. Lovely, right? However, at the onset of the visit, it doesn't usually feel so chivalrous. Now is the time to look and see what the good is here. Some examples could be that this critic just wants you to strive to be better, make sure you're not being lazy, only take on work that you can do at a high level of quality, etc. This may remind you of a well-meaning but dysfunctional aunt at a holiday dinner, but it's important to notice the underlying lesson.

The next step is to get that inner critic busy doing anything but bothering you. Give your saboteur a favorite hobby. When not in your knickers, what does it do for pure fun? Once its words of wisdom are deciphered and you are reminded of its good, you thank your inner critic and send it on its way to do the thing it most loves to do without you. It will leave gladly because whatever this other act is, it's super appealing to it. And then you re-enter your world with a lighter heart and more focus. You don't need to let the inner critic derail you.

Over time, you may discover more than one voice. Go through this exercise for each — they have different methods to their madness and varied lessons for you.

When I first learned this exercise, I quickly began to recognize my loudest inner critic. It was most often triggered whenever I sat down to read a novel, in which I wasn't going to learn anything, but rather engage in entertainment. The voice would say, "Why are you relaxing? You could be doing so many more productive things with your time, like a five-mile run."

When I heard this voice, all I could see was a big-haired version of myself from the '80s dressed in a Wonder Woman costume: hands on her hips, cape flowing behind her (even though I could not feel a breeze at all), with a stern face and voice. I named her Overactive Superhero. She couldn't stand the thought of me not accomplishing something at all times. Reading a novel for fun? Guffaw! She would rather see me exercising my good work ethic by bettering myself through other means. Roger that, Overactive Superhero! Thank you. Now, go on your way and do as many pull-ups as possible! And off she went, with a skip in her red-booted step.

Reflect on where you may hear this voice in various areas of your life, such as within your team, your community, your family, and your group of friends. We want to redefine your relationship with the inner critic through awareness, acceptance and powerful choice. As a reminder, here are the steps you should think to yourself:

- I will recognize the voice when I hear it.
- I will harvest the learnings, lessons, or protective message.
- I will send the inner critic on its way with gratitude.
- I will choose powerfully how I will play from this point forward, fully owning it.

The goal is to lessen the impact this voice has over you over time, not to stop it from showing up. You may hear it four, or even forty, times a day. Eventually it loses its mojo. The process is the same; it's a new dance to a familiar song. You are working with it, engaging in some gratitude, and taking your power back. All inner-game magic!

For a downloadable worksheet of this process, please see the resource section of my website: (http://www.livefullcoaching.com/book-buyers/).

In the next chapter we will use our inner compass to explore even further by identifying what's most important to us — our values.

CHAPTER 6
DEFINING AND LIVING YOUR VALUES

We are now aware of how our internal dialogue translates to external action. Let's get more specific about what's at the root of these feelings and triggers so that we are better able to navigate the tsunami of our day. For this purpose, I am intentionally leaving out any psychoanalyzing of your past. Instead, you can still be aware when things are off and how to address or honor them. In this chapter, we will explore the belief systems that get in the way of living fully and unapologetically, and learn how to use our values and beliefs as our compass for powerful choice.

As we covered in the previous chapter, our values are at the core of our being. A truly fulfilled state is one in which we make choices that are aligned with our values, the things that are most important to us. You may be tempted to judge others if their values are different from yours. You may find that you give your power away to, or retreat in a powerless way from, people who don't honor what's important to you. This could take the form of you blaming them for your unhappiness or allowing their actions to ruin your day. Honestly, the power of your happiness is not in anyone else's hands. It's up to you to create it and maintain it! All of these beliefs are helpful in the context of what we've already learned because, when you are wide awake with awareness, you are better able to choose how you want to act on your belief system.

I often have clients ask me for a list of values; this way, they can identify what's important to them. That may work well in a restaurant when you look at the menu and start to salivate at the options presented to you in written form. However, it's best to uncover your values more organically. Powerful, open-ended questions are a great way to uncover some emotions and triggers, as well as recognize the underpinning values.

Here are some questions I've asked new clients to help them unveil some values, which may lie at the heart of the answers.

- What is your biggest pet peeve?
- Under what circumstances do you find you are most judgmental?
- Tell me about the last time you snapped in anger or frustration at someone.

You may notice that those questions are on the edgy side, but I love them because those triggers are often close to the surface; you don't have to mine for them. There's knowledge for us in the dissonance that can help us to uncover our values.

When you have been living in stress and overwhelm with overpacked days and nights, it's easy to look for what's going wrong. In fact, you probably don't have to look at all; you are swatting away these instances like nasty, biting horse flies on a summer day. Rather than begrudge them, let's look at what they are telling you, similar to the public service announcement of your inner critic.

Perhaps your biggest pet peeve at work is when people say, "Yes, sure, I'll do it" with excitement and vigor, but then the results come in weeks later, after a missed deadline. What does the fact that this bothers you tell you about what is important to you? Perhaps you value punctuality, responsibility, follow-through, commitment, honesty. Or, is it something else? I like to write each thought out in a stream-of-consciousness exercise to see all the threads. The words themselves may mean different things to different people — only you will know what your writing means. The thought train on paper gives you more clarity.

Here are some questions on the flip side — not things that annoy you, but things that fulfill you — that may help you capture more of what's in your heart. This is the resonance.

- What was the proudest moment of your last year? Of your life thus far?
- If you had zero limitations of talent, time or treasure, what would your secret (or not-so-secret) dream be?
- If you could have a career other than this one, what would it be?
- Who is someone in your life that you admire? What characteristics of theirs do you want to emulate?

The same drill here applies to exploring your story and looking for the values that surface. Did your proudest moment in the last year involve work; say, a team project was completed with flying colors? Perhaps the underlying values are team engagement, completion, and recognition. If the proudest moment of your life was the birth of your first child, get clear on what value that honored. Was it family, love, or legacy?

I'll tell you a personal story that provides an example of how the same word or value can mean different things to different people. When I was at a coach training class shortly after the birth of my first daughter, we were discussing the peak moments in our lives in order to get clear on our values. I chose the experience of her birth, which was fresh for me — and I was pregnant again, about to engage in round two. One of my colleagues said that their own child's birth was their peak experience, too, and so we both said "family" was the primary value revealed by our children's birth stories.

When my colleague spoke more about her experience, she mentioned that family, for her, meant "the more the merrier," and that it is was particularly special to have her extended family in the room to witness the birth. I believe she said the birthing crew numbered in the double-digits. I thought I was going to have heart palpitations at the thought of it; that same experience of family, as she defined it, would not be fulfilling in my eyes. Having gone through IVF with way too much probing, prodding, and not enough privacy, the idea of a peanut gallery welcoming our little peanut was unacceptable. To me, family meant the intimacy of just my husband lovingly present. Yet, family was an equally special value to both of us, even though the details of what we meant by it were different.

As you explore the answers to these questions, drawing on examples from your work and home life, look for themes. You may notice that love comes up everywhere, or even that other concepts, such as family, honesty, work ethic, etc., keep reappearing. That's how you know you are ringing the tuning fork of values. Don't worry if you don't come up with a nice, neat list after journaling for ten minutes. The best way to catalog your values is to let your list grow organically over time. While the questions are provocative thought-starters, your real-life woes and whoas are going to give you more data immediately in the moment. In such moments, rewind to the lessons from Chapter Four that helped you to just notice your feelings. We can take this awareness a bit further and use it to tag a value.

If we were triggered by the rudeness of someone cutting us off on the freeway (you're listening to a member of the road rage club, right here), rather than just being aware that we are irritated, hot in the face, and likely screaming, look for and validate the value that has been violated inside you. When road rage visits me, it's usually the value of respect or consideration that I sense getting stepped on. Clearly, I'm judging the other driver without knowing the whole story. Perhaps they have a family emergency, or they have received terrible news and need to get somewhere ASAP.

Let's face it ... in the heat of the moment, we aren't receptive to their needs, nor are we detached from our acts. I promise, there's more to come later about how to handle and cope with the judgment monster. For now, use the trigger as data to identify an underlying value. That same value of respect that crashed on the road will be honored through another, more positive circumstance. We get to identify that when it surfaces, too.

For the purposes of this process, let's say we have a list now of about three to five values, knowing full well that the list will grow over time. It is possible to rank them in order of importance. This isn't necessary, as the importance might change over time or depending on the situation. What if two values compete with one another? Ah, the classic work life balance dance. You really care about follow-through and getting things done for your team on time. And, you really care about being a loving parent and attending the Scouts awards ceremony tonight. These value chains — follow-through, responsibility, love, family — they all matter to you. But how will you choose?

This is where I'm a huge fan of the short-term decision and putting your finger on the pulse of your values at any given moment to decide which one takes precedence. What is most important to you today? What will win your attention in this example — the Scouting event or the deliverables? Trust your heart and your amazing brain — it will work out no matter what. When you choose powerfully, you are no longer a victim to the circumstance, and you are most certainly not on autopilot. When life is running you, you aren't in charge. Tell that to your perfectionist saboteur! Slow down to go faster. When the friction of competing values has you chaffed and raw, look at what's most important today, in the short term.

In this case of Scouts vs. deliverables, Scouts may win out by nature of the importance of the award ceremony. If it was a regular den meeting, perhaps you'd send a proxy to help out. And the deliverables will get done, just maybe later in the night or the next day. Time to recontract with yourself, your family, and your internal clients on expectations, one decision at a time.

I love short-term decisions that honor values because you get to decide what value to honor in that moment vs. having to decide forever about only one value. I also like to change my mind. This is why I don't have any tattoos (this is not a judgment of tattoos at all, by the way — I just know me). If I'm honest with myself, when it comes to the seemingly whimsical moments, I don't want to laminate the plan. You may disagree, and that's okay with me, yet

I offer this freedom of choice to give your burned-out brain a break from always committing to things that may not serve you.

Outside of awareness and naming values in isolation, you get to view these values as part of your inner GPS or your compass of sorts. Once I realized that my top two values are freedom and flexibility, I look at every decision through those lenses. I feel so much more fulfilled when I'm honoring these values than when structure is put in place. Remember, I like to change my mind, so a job, or hobby, or any task that requires extreme, inflexible routine is not my jam. I used to be a commodity trader, and the routine of brokers calling, market opening, trading, market closing, books, etc. was a mini prison for me. For others, this is their dream come true. I say, to each their own. Focus on what's important to you and take inventory of what decisions you are making that are aligned with your values.

There are times when freedom doesn't win in my playbook. Those circumstances are rare, but you bet I'm walking around wide awake about the cases in which I made the powerful choice to override it. And, when I choose, I allow myself full ownership, which then feels less like a trade-off and more like a decision.

That's one of the myth-buster ideas I want you to play with regarding work life balance. Achieving it requires an inner-game focus and mindfulness shift. As long as you approach balance aware that you can't have it all — you have to give something up to get something else — that's exactly how you are going to experience your life. For example, if you feel like you need to skip dessert because you didn't run that day to burn it off, check in about whether that decision feels obligatory or if it feels like a good trade-off. Put on your big girl pants and decide. Say to yourself, "I'm choosing this — this dessert, this job, this partner — because I'm honoring a value." Be clear what that value is. Zero victims here. Bravo!

Sometimes, you'll have a very visceral reaction to a decision. You know it doesn't feel right, but you do it anyway. How did that work out? My plea to you is to slow the clock down and temper others' expectations of you until you take the pulse of your values. The reality is that you're going to pay now or pay later, and my wish for you is to be sure you are winning because the ripple effect of your fulfillment will pay dividends.

What if neither decision feels good? What if leaving work early feels terrible and skipping Scouts feels terrible, too? Then decide what value to honor in that moment, knowing full well there will be many other decisions before the sun sets, and with them opportunities to make different choices. This is a call to action to stop being a victim and be the victor of your values, one moment at a time. Make a mistake? No sweat. Decide differently next time.

This may all sound like I'm telling you, "Suck it up, buttercup." But really, I'm just asking you to trust this process. And if you can't trust it blindly, then start behaving differently and get the evidence yourself.

I know it may feel like an uncomfortable stretch from what you may be used to — navigating the rat race on autopilot. Please be kind to yourself in this process. If you are judging roadblocks and mishaps, you are less likely to see this through. Look at the learnings through a curious eye because curiosity and judgment cannot coexist. Try it! Question whether you are really curious, or if you are just looking for evidence to support the story in your head that you already believe. You'll always find what you are looking for.

I often talk to my clients about being "one you." Don't wear a mask at work and then rip it off on the car ride home in place of another mask (no pun intended during a global pandemic). Who are you truly? This authentic you is the person who honors their values unapologetically. Stop trying to impress the sheep. You need to impress yourself first by realizing what turns you on and taps you in. Then, do more of that.

Distress vs. Eustress

Sometimes clients will engage in coaching because their manager said they need to change. Feedback is a gift — it's optional to take it and it's up to you what you do with it. 360 surveys of the sort used in many corporate environments, along with other surveys, can be very impactful in that they help disclose blind spots and hidden strengths. But, like anything, there are pros and cons to them. I want to be clear that by the end of our executive life coaching retainer, the client is ideally more authentic and dialing up the volume of their values even more.

Have you ever heard that you'd be even better if you just weren't so much of you? Well, I have heard this. I'm too loud, too optimistic, too extroverted, too whatever. That feedback used to sting. But now, through coaching with self-love, awareness, and acceptance, I'm powerfully choosing who I want to be based on my values, and it's flipping awesome. I want this for you! I want you to stop hiding. I want you to stop being a people-pleaser or a rescuer and focus that same energy on your own authenticity. The world will win when you win! And you can't win if you are a confused thespian in life, trying to figure out what role to play when. Just be you — all of you.

The salmon swims up stream for survival. I get it. And, unless one of your values is struggle, then honoring your values becomes your compass to navigate the waters of life in a more fulfilling way. You may want to be challenged, and you know that some of the most rewarding experiences are tough. As a three-time natural childbirth vet, I fully agree. I'm speaking of the difference between distress and eustress.

Going back to the example of the salmon, I'm sure that if I was an ESPN announcer for the great salmon run in Alaska, and I could chat with one of the fish on their upward path to spawn, they'd likely be distressed because their survival depends on it. If we want to not just survive, but we want to thrive, we can get there through moments of fulfilling challenge too. Eustress is that positive stress you feel before an exciting challenge. It's the feeling you get during moments like the beginning of a race, or before you step on stage to speak at the sales conference. The heart still pounds out of your chest, your breath is shallow and racing, and the exhilaration that accompanies it and the met goal is worth the rush.

If you'd like a more in-depth worksheet on how to clarify values and make decisions accordingly, see the reference page in the back of this book, or visit my website: (http://www.livefullcoaching.com/book-buyers/). We will learn further tools to help us thrive even more as we continue. The next chapter will put you in the driver's seat allowing you, more than ever before, to live this life fully.

CHAPTER 7
YOU ARE THE BOSS OF YOU

It's time to dial up the volume on powerful choice with you as the number one client of these decisions. For all of you real-life action figures out there, this chapter is a game-changer. It's time to take your power back, in terms of both actions and perspective. In this chapter, you will learn and apply tools to shift your inner game, inspire your outer game actions, and create structures and boundaries for self-care.

Maybe you have measured your success based on what you've accomplished or accumulated up to this point. Or, maybe you've measured it by what your boss or others at work have recognized in you. I'm inviting you to redefine what success looks like by taking on energy as the new metric. What does this mean? It means your personal energy level (before, during and after action) is the new measure of success. How do you feel when you are making decisions, when you are setting that goal or making that list? How do you feel during the project or as you're taking action? How do you feel once it's complete? While there are shades of grey in these responses, there is really one question you can ask yourself to determine if you are on the right track: does what you're doing drain you or fuel you?

Your self-care and related energy levels are the most important things you can focus on right now. Ever try driving a car with no fuel? Even the gasless Tesla needs a snazzy recharge station. What is your equivalent of recharging and refueling? Even before our gauges scream "empty," what are we doing day in and day out that robs us of our energy? It's time to say "no" to more and more of those things, or to do them creatively with a new perspective. Stephen Covey, author of *7 Habits of Highly Effective People*, encouraged readers to exercise the habit of "sharpening the saw." We cannot keep doing the things, like sawing, if we do not take time to recharge ourselves, or sharpen the tool. We all know these things intellectually, but we haven't practiced enough to develop the muscle memory we need. If we had, we wouldn't be chatting about burnout.

Let's start with the decision to say no. One option could be to outright amputate the task and take it off your plate completely by delegating, renegotiating, or any number of other strategies that would end your energy drain. You might disagree. You may think that when you've been "voluntold" to do something at work, or when the business situation requires you to take certain measures, that you are no longer in a place of choice. Furthermore, your belief system around saying no could paralyze you, preventing you from taking any action other than begrudgingly moving forward.

There are better ways to approach the situation.

Let's take an example from the home first. Personally speaking, I do not excel at cleaning and organizing. It drains the life out of me, and I prefer to say no whenever possible in order to preserve my energy for things I do enjoy, such as budgeting (yes, it's true!). So, for me, I delegate these activities to service providers or "barter" time for services. If you can hire someone to help you, do so. If money is an issue, swap favors with a friend or a loved one who is super good at this type of thing. For every excuse that you can come up with, I guarantee there is a suitable solution.

But, just for fun, let's pretend there is no solution. You are stuck doing your version of the grunt job. There are ways to make it more bearable or even fun. When I'm doing an unpleasant task like organizing or cleaning, I put ear buds in and jam out to my tunes like nobody's biz. There is something about music plugged right into my eardrums that drowns out the woes and dials up the "woo-hoos!"

Therefore, I choose to make cleaning more fun or at least more enjoyable. I'm less drained this way, even though the task is a perceived necessity for me at the moment. Although the "what" goes on, it is the "how" I choose to tackle the chore that energizes me.

From a work perspective, we are too often handed objectives, projects or lists that are not our own, and we feel the need to comply. My wish for you here is to realize that you decide the "what" and the "how" each step of the way. Don't believe you can say no to the boss? Remember, you are the boss of you.

Let's play this out. As an example, imagine your boss has demanded you reduce headcount while still maintaining the current workload on your team.

Some people may be jazzed by such actions, but let's pretend that you are unhappy about them. Putting the dipstick in your oil tank of energy, things are looking low and dark. You may think you have no choice but to execute as planned. But you are likely underestimating your brainpower. By brainpower, I mean your intellectual ability in addition to your ability to choose your thoughts that then turn into actions. The more negative your thoughts and perspective, the more negative the tasks and experience. Lucky for us all, the opposite is true as well. The more positive your thoughts and perspective, the more positive the tasks and experience.

Now, break it down. What are the specific parts of this assignment that drain you? For example, maybe you find it hard to communicate to others that they are no longer on the team (or worse, no longer employed). Perhaps you have a hard time with disappointing others, so you'd rather work fourteen hours a day than say no to someone. Perhaps the thought of not delivering to the company pains you, since you value contribution and performance. Perhaps all of the above (or some new set of unnamed scenarios) empties you of your energy. Pay attention to the specifics and look below the surface to understand why they sting. There's gold there!

Ask yourself, "What can I chunk down and delegate or say no to?" Using the example above for headcount, how could you partner with Human Resources or others to communicate player changes? Who else is really good at this who can coach you, mentor you, or even tag team with you? Is there another creative way to handle the situation?

When maintaining the current workload and operating business as usual, find where you can you say, "No, not yet, not now." There may be others who have the strengths in this area who can pick up special projects or responsibilities (inside or outside your team). What can you renegotiate so that it feels good? Consider the triangle of time, money, and resources (e.g., human capital). If one of the sides of the triangle changes, the others are impacted. For example, if a timeline is shortened, how we increase investment of money or of human capital to make that happen early? As a leader, you get to analyze and negotiate these decisions and related impacts.

Remember, it doesn't matter what I included or omitted as possible scenarios. What matters is that you ask yourself some powerful, open-ended questions that do not have a yes or no answer and that you then check in with each potential solution. As you weigh each scenario, pretend that that is the route you have decided to take and assess your energy level. Has it improved? What could make the situation even better, easier, more energizing?

I know you don't want to disappoint anyone. But consider this: if you are exhausted and performing subpar because of it, your chances of disappointing others are higher anyway. And if work is taking a toll on your personal life, does it matter how much you are "winning" at the office if you are unhappy all the time? Think of it this way — you are disappointing yourself, and you are your number one client. If you are happy, everything will fall into place a lot more easily, more quickly, and in a way that leaves you with more energy.

Now that you've explored all the options, let's pretend you still must proceed with the task, no "nos" allowed. I know, I know. I just walked you through all of these options. However, I want to show you what's possible, even when you think or feel you don't have a choice.

The next step is to think about what type of perspective shifts you could make. As long as you are in dread or drain, that is exactly how you'll experience all related activities. But if you try on a new perspective for a while, like test-driving a new car before you buy it, you'll see that there's a novel experience to be had on the same commute to work. Here are some questions to mine for a new perspective:

- What is the gift for me or for others in this experience?
- How can this be easier than I imagine?

- Where is the fun, the energy here?
- How can this experience be my greatest teacher?

You are limitless with this approach, but you should look for a new lens and peer through it. For example, let's consider the example of letting team members go to reduce headcount.

What is the gift? Perhaps there's an opportunity to address talent issues or to provide an opening for people to pursue another passion of theirs by going elsewhere.

How can this be easier than I imagine? What if you tapped into others who can mentor you through this? Perhaps you could even delegate the task to someone. It may be better for you to choose to experience this circumstance from the sidelines rather than playing an active role because it is a temporary challenge.

Where is the fun, the energy here? Maybe the fun-factor isn't at an all-time high, but what may provide more energy is to honor these folks and express your gratitude for their service. Perhaps finding the ways, words, and timing that feel best for you is how you'll harvest more energy.

How can this be my greatest teacher? Somehow this is happening for you, not to you. You may never look forward to these events, but there's always something to learn through the process. For example, new perspectives of transparency, empathy, or skilled communication.

There's always a solution that serves you if you believe it to be true. As long as you are in the perspective that this is "it" and that "it" sucks, it surely will. So, you can change the action or change your perspective. Either way, you get more of what you focus upon. Why not choose a better-feeling thought or action?

Self-care: Selfish or Self-serving?

You may be in the camp of the people I work with who says, "taking care of me is selfish." Perhaps you work incredibly long hours, commute an insane distance, or have a global job that never sleeps. In that case, I can imagine that the thought of taking more time away from your work obligations or family is simply selfish in your mind. It could be that, over the years, it has been engrained in you that you must put others before yourself (after all, that's what "good" soldiers do). Maybe you have parental or spousal guilt if you engage in me time outside of the semi-annual vacation (when you are likely logged on or plugged in anyway).

Truth smack! I'm happy to shout from the hillside that *not* taking care of you is selfish. Why do I speak such tomfoolery? Because you have nothing of quality to give in the long run to your business, personal life, or this planet when you are unhappy, stressed, ill, drained, or fried. You may think your colleagues and family are getting the best of you ... but for how long? And what's left?

Here's your new mantra: *Taking care of me isn't selfish, it's self-serving*. Remember, when you win, everyone wins. That's right, boys and girls! Step right up and get your ticket to the Self-service Show.

I personally went through twelve years of Catholic school, so putting myself first took a ton of reprogramming and I still need reminding. No offense to my religious upbringing, but it wasn't exactly popular to engage in "self" of any sort. Add that background to my need to please, over-give and contribute in the workplace and in my whole life, and it was a recipe for burnout.

I often turn to nature for the perfect example of self-care and cycles. We need the dormancy of winter in order for the world to bud in spring and thrive in summer. At nighttime, flowers close their blooms, and the diurnal animals sleep in order to recharge. It's natural, it's normal, it's needed. When our brains, egos and external influences get in the way, we buck this normalcy.

You need to recharge in the workplace, too. Even our sleepless global roles need to nap every day. You get to decide how you take these breaks, but some examples would include:

- Actually take a "lunch hour" to eat or walk. (*Geez!*)
- Don't log on after the kids go to sleep. (*Gasp!*)
- Do something "fun" during weeknights. (*Guffaw!*)
- Work no weekends, assuming you are not on call. (*Gulp!*)

I don't care if you do all of these things, some hybrid of them, or create your own set of self-care practices. Just start doing something that feels good to you and stop doing the things that don't.

I understand the sun never sleeps, but, then again, it's a big flaming star that is doomed to burn out at some point. You, on the other hand, are planted on this earth and need to rest and recharge like every other living thing on this planet. Cycles, baby. It's all about cycles.

Now, it's not all bad news. At times, our drive and values are honored in some way when we tackle things that eventually drain us. We discussed values at length in the last chapter. It's when you are allowing everything else to dictate how you spend your time at the expense of your energy level that you are engaging in a disservice to yourself, and, as a result, everyone around you.

I want you to take inventory of your current belief system around self-care by ranking them on a scale of 1 to 10, 1 being not at all, 10 being "hell yes":

- I feel guilty when I take time for me.
- I don't have time to take care of myself.
- I don't have the money to take care of myself.
- I don't have a support system (e.g., significant other, work culture, childcare, etc.) to allow me to take care of myself.

Look for some themes in your answers. Where are your biggest challenges? Where are your strengths? If you take a look back at the Wheel of Life, you might see strengths to leverage. For example, for many executives I coach, money is not an issue. Therefore, they can throw some coin towards a solution such as hiring a trainer for their much-needed workouts or a babysitter so that they can take a mini-vacation.

If work culture is your obstacle, I will reiterate that you are the boss of you. How you create this time or perception shift is in your hands. It's while waiting for other things to change that you lose yourself and your choice. Just claim it! In this day and age, especially for the millennial generation, seeking work life balance is more accepted. Of course, there are deadlines, team meetings, and other obligations. I'm not advising you to ignore all of that. I am saying that where there's a will, there's a way.

There are tools in this chapter and on the resource page to help this become even more real for you. One of these is a Self-Care Calendar to help you plan out on a daily, weekly, monthly, quarterly and yearly cadence. For a downloadable worksheet of this process, please see the resource section of my website: (http://www.livefullcoaching.com/book-buyers/).

Healthy Boundaries

I want to explore boundaries with you. You may be feeling the pain of current boundaries or constraints in your life. And, hopefully, you are embracing some ways to deal with those. For the purpose of this section, boundaries are our friend. They are the foundation for the structure of self-care that we are erecting. They are the walls of the pool, so that we can swim freely in our newly defined, self-care waters. They are the guardrails that help us stay away from the cliffs from which there is no return. This is where we apply "no" in the form of structures that help us stay in the self-service lane on the highway of life.

I encourage many of my corporate clients to tap into where their energy is the highest and lowest during the day. Then, they can block out those times in their online calendars as "sacred time." Not a morning person? Don't allow meetings before 9:30 a.m. Burned out by 4 p.m.? Have a no-meeting zone after 3:30 p.m. Now, I completely understand when things pop up and people invite you to everything under the sun. Remember to check in with your energy level. Ask yourself, "Is this draining or unnecessary?" Then, say "no" or delegate. Is this a game-changing must-do? Make an exception and purposefully say "yes," invoking the powerful choice that you will borrow from sacred time and bring the new perspective along with it.

If you are permitting the daily "river dance" all over your sacred time, then you are allowing everyone to rule your calendar. There's only one person responsible for this, and that is you. If you are totally cool with it, then that's okay because you are truly not drained. But be honest with yourself and know your boundaries and intolerances.

T-Tool

Sometimes we are still stuck emotionally. All the happy affirmations written in lipstick on the mirror aren't going to magically change anything. This next tool I'm going to share has been critical to my own shifts as well as those of my clients. It's a process that was developed by Rebecca Hanson and is called the T-Tool; I have used it with my clients for years after I visited Rebecca's Law of Attraction training center. She has since retired, yet I have her permission to use this game-changing process.

1. Choose a topic on which you feel stuck and would like to feel differently.
2. Draw a big, capital T on a letter-sized piece of paper.
3. At the top of the page, write a topic.
4. Write "I don't want/don't like feeling" on the top left-side of the T
5. Underneath, create a bulleted list of all the feelings related to this topic that you no longer want to feel. Go until you can no longer think of one more.
6. On the top, right-hand side, write "I do want/do like feeling."

7. For each bullet on the left, list on the right how you want to feel instead.
8. Draw a big letter "X" through the Don't Want side and fold the paper in half so that you can only see the Do Wants.
9. Say the following three affirmations for each bullet:
   - "I am in the process of ..."
   - "Higher Power/Universe/God ... is in the process of ..."
   - "I love it when ..."

Here is an example. Let's say you are stuck in a perspective about your boss. You are feeling overmanaged and underappreciated, work is a drag, and you think, "If I just didn't report to him, life would be so much better." The reality is that you cannot control this immediate reporting relationship unless you leave your job. You cannot control what he does, but you can control what you do. If you are not ready or willing to leave, or are unsure, then change your inner game and take your power back.

The topic at the top would read "relationship with boss." On the left, some "Don't Want" feelings may include *micro-managed, unappreciated, undervalued, stuck, frustrated*, etc. Once these are all captured, the reframe column on the right could read *empowered, appreciated, recognized, free, peaceful*, respectively. Remember to say the positive, not "not this". It is very important. After writing all of the reframes, draw an "X" through the left list and practice the three statements with each new bullet. Feel the difference after just one sitting! The more you practice, the more you will notice the shifts becoming quick, easy, and sustainable.

The only time I find that this doesn't work is when a client really isn't ready to shift. In that case, they are still married to their perspective and aren't prepared to move on. Remember, the question from earlier: do you want to be right or do you want to heal? When you are ready to heal, try this out, and let the shift hit the fan.

You can download this worksheet on the resources page of my website: (http://www.livefullcoaching.com/book-buyers/).

Goal setting

We have focused quite a bit on the inner game, and all of your best external actions will come from this new grounded, aligned place. Had we started to set goals and take action without doing this work first, you would only see a small amount of movement. But now we're ready to try out a goal-setting exercise with our revised mindset and a new method to help goals come to life.

As corporate warriors, you have likely seen or used some version of SMART objectives (specific, measurable, attainable, realistic and time-bound). You can visit the resources page for the history of its evolution. At CTI, I learned there is a more stimulating version, the backwards version called TRAMS, to get engaged with goal setting.

T (thrilling): What is thrilling about pursuing this objective in the first place? What is the process of pursuing it, and what will final completion look like? Looking for the thrill is so important. The typical approach of "just do it" can feel flat and unmotivating.

R (resonance): This is where your values come in! What values are honored when you pursue this objective? After all of the work we did on values, you can see how important it is to connect the dots and find out how the objective you're seeking honors who you truly are.

A (accountability): Who is the person that is your champion as you pursue this objective? We aren't talking about the whip-cracker who yells at you when things get tough, but rather a person who is lifting you up no matter what.

M (metrics): This is where you'll put down the criteria for success that you would normally list during a typical goal-setting exercise. How will you know when this task is completed successfully? As we learned earlier, adding in a metric for energy level will dial this up even more.

S (specifics): How will we make progress on this goal? What is the specific strategy and its related steps? This helps map out the plan to move forward.

Compare this strategy with your usual method of corporate goal setting and note the difference. You may doubt that such an optimistic objective setting as TRAMS is applicable in the work world. But I know firsthand that it works: I piloted this strategy when I was the HR head of a startup company, and it helped people shift and think about their mental and heart connection to an objective — much more than typical SMART exercises do.

Let's use a work example of a mandatory objective to cut your budget by 30 percent. Typically, any budget decrease has people emotionally charged in some way. For the sake of this example, let's say you are not a fan of this objective and are having a hard time engaging with vigor. Even if this objective was cascaded down with sound business logic, you may still feel resistance. Here is an example of TRAMS for this case.

T (thrill) – While this may not feel thrilling right now, I can find the thrill in engaging with some thought partners who are good at this and who can help me think outside of my current paradigm. It also feels thrilling to have completed a challenge through creative means.

R (resonance) – It honors my loyalty value to the team and the company to create a budget that meets everyone's needs including my own. I feel as if I'm honoring freedom as well since I can say no to the things that are not mission-critical or do not have the best ROI for the company. I will do this in a way that honors my integrity and responsibility values so that I show up as a powerful leader in service of the company.

A (accountability) – I will ask Paul, as he has navigated this successfully in the past, and he'll be a good champion for me during this thought process.

M (metrics) – The SWB (salary, wages and benefits), spending projections, project scope, etc. will be met by the deadline (specific to this objective).

S (specifics) – Conduct bi-weekly meetings with a traffic light scorecard approach to the above metrics until the deadline that is 90 days out.

For a downloadable worksheet, please see the resource section of my website: (http://www.livefullcoaching.com/book-buyers/).

Hopefully you have experienced some shifts as we are going along, and the actions you are putting in place stem from a more authentic, aligned you. While it's quite empowering to be the Boss of You, we will take even more pressure off in the next chapter by broadening your support system with the ultimate team player: your Higher Power.

CHAPTER 8
YOUR BEST CO-PILOT

When you are feeling like you are running out of time and your to-do list is ticking higher than a progressive jackpot on a slot machine, life can be a very lonely place. It is important to remember that we are not alone on this planet. We always have someone, such as a friend, a family member, a co-worker, or perhaps we are blessed with many of each. And there is the most important player on your team, to whom you always have access: you may call it God, Source, A Higher Power, the Universe, Infinite Intelligence, Collective Consciousness, Energy, Law of Attraction, Mother Earth. Whatever it is for you, the odds are that your background and the environment in which you were raised led you to believe in something *bigger than you*. Even if you doubt this, I encourage you to read on. Maybe you'll even learn to trust in your Higher Self — the best, most grounded version of you — if you get nothing else from this chapter.

Just as you trust the navigation system in your car when you can't see how it operates, you are invited in this chapter to trust your Higher Power, however you define that term, and learn tools to help you tap in for guidance. I have some clients who are not of the spiritual mindset, so this is sometimes a challenge for them. I'd like to introduce you to the concept of the "Virtual Jerry Maguire," based on the titular character in the 1996 movie. You don't have to have seen this movie to understand what I mean. Here's what you need to know: In the film, Tom Cruise plays a sports agent who loses his job when he makes his personal mission statement public to his company. He also loses all of his clients — except one. His sole job becomes hanging on to his one and only client through over-the-top customer service to ensure that client gets what he needs and wants in his professional football contract.

Imagine you have a Virtual Jerry Maguire at your disposal. You delegate to your Life Agent, Jerry, what you want and need, and this support system is negotiating behind the scenes on your behalf to make it happen. You let go, and let Jerry, so to speak, work the magic. Your only job is to be crystal clear on what "good" looks and feels like for you. Once you've figured that out, let go of the resistance and don't worry too much about the details of how that goodness is going to be achieved. Trust it will work out.

I was privileged to see Dr. Wayne Dyer speak a few times, and I even met him at a "Writing From Your Soul" workshop in Maui, the summer before he left this physical world. He always spoke of *ego* as an acronym for "Edging God Out." I think of this often when I'm feeling like it's all on me to get it done, to succeed, to do things. When I forget I have a powerhouse of a resource on my team, I get very overwhelmed, stressed, and worried. The ego is a very real thing, but we don't need to give it so much power. We can use the ego voice to remind us that we've gone astray from who we truly are. So, instead of edging God out (or however you define your Higher Power), you have the opportunity to lean in and delegate to the Universe, so to speak.

As I mentioned in the last chapter, I was raised Catholic, and my upbringing as a Christian has taught me certain things about faith and trust. As my viewpoints have evolved, I see things more broadly than ever. It wasn't until my adult years that I learned about the Law of Attraction and energy healing. (I'll talk a bit more about these concepts later.) No matter what your beliefs are, this chapter is not designed to convince you of one thing or another. It is intended to be more of an invitation to get beyond the doing of the things and shift towards being. And part of what allows you to do that is the *unseen*. We can trust our navigation system in our cars to get us from Point A to Point B, even though we can't see how it works. We can also trust in the powers that be to lead us in our whole lives, even as we lead at work.

My go-to resource on the topic, Abraham-Hicks, gives this key principal of The Law of Attraction: *That which is like unto itself, is drawn*. In other words, you get results where you focus, whether those results are wanted or unwanted. If you are thinking, speaking, feeling, or doing something with a certain mindset, you are aligning with that outcome. The saying "birds of a feather flock together" is one way to think about how this works. Once we understand this universal law, we can use it to our advantage. Whether you are new to the Law of Attraction or have been practicing for years, there are many resources to go more in depth on the concept; feel free to use the materials listed in the resource guide at the end of this book and at my website to do more reading: (http://www.livefullcoaching.com/book-buyers/).

We've already learned a few tools that, whether you realized it or not, may have tapped into a Higher Power, such as the T-tool that uses an affirmation about your "Higher Power" to shift your vibe. This is a way to get connected to how you are feeling and what you want and to let go or delegate at the same time. We do the work and so does Source, God or Higher Power when we let go and let God. It's like we are doing the work by putting the seeds in the ground, covering with soil and watering, yet there is also something behind the scenes contributing to the growth that is not in our direct control. This is how we get to be in action while we are supported from Source at the same time.

Personally, I find delegation to a Higher Power very refreshing because it gives me a chance to let go of feeling like I can control everything by myself 100 percent of the time. Often, I feel like I need to be in action in order to make progress. How can just being get me anywhere? Think back to what I mentioned earlier with the Overactive Superhero. It's tempting to feel we have to be the living Nike commercial — continually "just doing it" — or else we stagnate. In my older years, I've learned that slowing down and being mindful helps me to go faster. It is way more helpful than the grind I was used to.

It's really a "yes" to all of it. Say "yes" to the being and doing and also to the delegating. From this place you can act and trust with confidence. Delegation to God or the Universe doesn't mean you just sit back, direct, and judge the outcomes without taking any responsibility. That doesn't seem like your style, anyway, as control and action are in your DNA. It's a shift, however, to enroll the best team member you'll ever have, as you continue to live and work towards your goals.

Personally, I love list making. I write on sticky notes and put them up everywhere. One day, I had an idea to create custom "to be" and "to do" sticky notes. I found that only by connecting with the being-state first could I create a to-do list that was aligned with my goals. By being-state I mean intention or mindset. When I didn't get connected with my mind and heart first, the list I created was a frantic run-on of everything personal, such as laundry, field trip permission slips, and vet visits. Or, the list would become all about business: taxes, invoicing, and client calls. Yes, it all had to get done at this moment, or so I thought (prioritization is another topic). But there was no room to breathe, zero intention put into my day. And then, the autopilot pace of my day would take over, and stress would ensue. Slowing down to think about my intention — and how I wanted to be — changed everything.

For example, if I had a day packed with clients, I wanted to be present and service-minded. Connecting with those intentions naturally helped me prioritize, so that I wasn't distracted or led by ego but, rather, focused in a servant leadership mindset to make a difference for my clients. If I had a day packed with kid-related activities, I wanted to be patient, caring, and present. I don't necessarily need patience with my clients, but I personally need it with my young ones and the dynamics of all they bring. For me, being present with my family is key because I tend to drift off about the business to-do list or personal chores if I'm not intentional. Remember intention versus expectation — as discussed in Chapter Five — applies here also.

It only takes a minute to set a "to be" intention, and this can be done in the beginning of each day through sticky notes, journaling, or meditation. Or, intentions can be set in the beginning of each new meeting or player change. For example, if you know you are heading into a meeting with people who you typically trigger you, take a breath and write down or say how you want to be. For example, you could be curious, supportive, accepting, assertive, or anything that helps you get intentional. Let's say you show up miserably anyway, regardless of your intention. You can still learn from that experience and try again next time. Be kind to yourself; you are attempting to break old habits for the new. I bet you'll show up better and more powerfully than you imagined.

Transitions are a great time to set your intentions or how you want "to be. "When I commuted 40 minutes each way in my corporate days, I'd use this time to ramp up and wind down in the car with music or some mindfulness, in order to leave one world for another. Now that my commute is ten yards from office to main house, I have a ritual I do as I clean up my desk to end that world and begin the mom life again. The gratitude of the day, the list of follow-ups for tomorrow, and the reset of the "to be" from home begins. Without it, things are way more chaotic.

Another way to be more mindful throughout the day (besides formal transition times) is through a mindfulness timer or bell of sorts. I use Mindful Mynah, (see resource guide), the Breethe app, or the Calm app but there are plenty of options out there, including the alarm on your smartphone or laptop. The goal is to set the alarm with some frequency and use it to remind you to take deep breaths. Remember your intention at the beginning of the day or task.

When I'm writing, I set the mindfulness bell every fifteen minutes to keep me focused and on task. Regardless of whether I have a full day with clients or a day off, I'll set it every hour. I actually love when it goes off in the middle of a meeting because I'll rope in whoever is with me to breathe along. Everyone wins with that purposeful breath! Even if you didn't set an intention for the day, the deep breathing a few rounds is wonderful for mindfulness and to get grounded in the present.

Meditation has played an important role in my life and that of my clients. However, it's often met with a lot of resistance. People will say, "I can't just sit there and think of nothing!" I hear that quite frequently. Meditation isn't necessarily mindlessness ... it's allowing thoughts to visit and keep on moving like clouds in the sky or leaves drifting down the stream in autumn.

There are plenty of gurus, books, apps and classes that can help you learn more about mindfulness and meditation. Either way, try a free app or set the timer as we discussed in Chapter Four, when we went over square breathing. See how it benefits your decision making afterwards. Try this in the morning or at night to start, and then midday when you truly don't think you have any time to do it. Set the bar low and do the doable for five minutes when you feel the day getting away from you.

A few of these tools like the "to be" list, intention setting, mindfulness, and meditation are all ways to receive some form of Divine Guidance, or energy, to uplift you in your life. When we are too busy living and doing, there's no room to receive. Like I've said before, nature has found a way of creating balance: ocean tides go in and out, the sun rises and sets. We, too, need to receive just as much as we give.

Try getting quiet and journaling while musing over a powerful question like "what do I need to know right now?" Let the pen write the thoughts that come to mind. You'll get gold nuggets of knowledge. Your pen will write fast but not fast enough for your thoughts. It will be simple; Divine Guidance is rarely complicated. It won't do your power point presentation for you, but it will lead you to making more inspired choices.

Law of Attraction

You may have heard of the book *The Secret*, which introduced many to the Law of Attraction, or learned about it from somewhere else such as Abraham-Hicks. Maybe you are a huge fan, or maybe you are a total skeptic. I invite you to consider that you get where you vibrate. What does that mean? Our emotions have vibrations associated with them, and our emotions also draw vibration to us. Have you been in a funk and you just knew the day wasn't going to go well? Perhaps you had that thought right when you got out of bed. The events that followed gave you further evidence for your conclusion: squabbles at work, coffee spilled on your shirt, etc. Unfortunately, you played a role in creating all of that because of the way in which you were vibrating. We don't always get what we want, but we do get where we focus. It's as real as gravity.

Take love, for example. Ever hear someone say that they just can't find love, even though they are looking everywhere? By the nature of looking everywhere, they are telling the Universe (and reminding themselves) that they don't have it, and that just brings more lack, more gap. Once we shift our thoughts and feelings, our vibration follows suit.

I've given you some examples already of how the Law of Attraction has shifted aspects of my life. Think of the example of my drying-up well: using gratitude to shift my feelings from focusing on what I lacked to focusing on what I had in abundance changed my vibration: I allowed and received wealth. I didn't *do* anything else differently. I didn't chase the money, and I didn't put effort into marketing or drumming up sales. Any actions, even the non-actions, were divinely inspired from a place of trust, grounding, and already-doneness. Once I stopped putting in all that unnecessary effort and trusted myself and my Higher Power, things looked up.

This is the same with any topic, and all of the tools that we have learned up to this point will help you manifest what you are looking for, including more time for fun, self-care, and passions in your life. When you keep saying you have no time, you are bringing more "no time" into your life.

Someone once told me that the Universe is like a big Google search engine. It doesn't recognize when you say "no" or "don't want," it only responds to where you focus. For example, if you type "no porn" into the search engine, what do you think is going to show up? Given this could be on a work computer, let's try something less risky, such as "no furniture." I can make the same point without you receiving a visit from Compliance at your desk. The Universe is a giant search engine. Use it wisely.

We are not alone. We are not living in a silo, disconnected from everything else around us. We are all co-creating what is here, so let's play a responsible part in how we show up. I don't mean this in a political or environmental way, although it's completely translatable to any topic. It relates to our inner game, our outer game, and a Higher Power all working on our behalf.

Regardless of your personal and spiritual beliefs, I hope you remember that you are not alone and that there's more power you can leverage to help you live your best, unapologetic life. This next chapter will explore how to expand your life leadership team to include these tools and to further use inner, outer and upper games to create the life you love at work and home.

CHAPTER 9
YOUR UNAPOLOGETIC LIFE

Take a look at your own company or other large companies and philanthropies that have a Board of Directors. This board is composed of a variety of players, all of whom come with different backgrounds and viewpoints, and offer a plethora of advice and perspectives to help the organization reach decisions for the greater good. We have met a few players from your world throughout this book. Most notably, you have met (and maybe named) your inner critic and your Higher Power. Think of yourself as building a board of directors for you, a whole Life Leadership Team.

When you think back to any big decisions in your life that you've made following consultation with others, who was on your short list of trusted colleagues? Who is the one person you always run decisions by before making a move? Even if they have left this physical world, who did you go to or tap into for guidance? Perhaps it's a former sports coach, a college teacher, a work mentor, a parent. What about family, friends, or that frenemy you know would give you a devil's advocate perspective?

Another way to think about the people is to look back at your core values and ask, "Who would best represent this for me?" A Board can often be quite helpful because they are helping you see all of the different aspects of a situation or problem or opportunity to provide a synergistic solution.

On my Life Leadership Team, I have both of my parents, who offer very different but important skills to sense-check my decision making. My father is very logical and analytical, and he will steer me towards practicality and safety. My mother will also want me to be safe, but she leads with her heart and would steer me towards what I'm passionate about. There are many others on my board, including my saboteur and Higher Power. I'm very clear about the role they each play.

Let's get started putting yours together. Take a piece of paper and draw a large oval on it. This is your boardroom table. Start to write down who is on your Life Leadership Team (LLT), filling the seats around the table. Shoot for eight to ten names, but trust whoever your gut is telling you is right. For this exercise, include your inner critic and Higher Power in seats because they each play a different role.

What are you noticing about the players? What specific reasons did you pick to have them on your LLT? Just like all boards, there will be some decision making that needs to happen according to the bylaws. For this purpose, I'd suggest that you are the decision maker, but that you solicit input from other members. With your leadership role in mind, look back at the table seating. What's missing here, or what changes might you need to make considering the greater good — *your* greater good?

You are the client of this process, no one else. So, there are zero pity invites to the table — not an in-law who you think would pout in the real world if they felt left out. There is no room for an obligatory seat on your Life Leadership Team!

What kind of rules would you like to put in place? These are the bylaws of your LLT. We know the first rule is that you make all final decisions, but what else is important to you? Perhaps you put a time limit on consultations with the board, or you give more weight to your Higher Power than to your saboteur. Remember, they all have a service to provide, so it behooves you to consider all points before the final decision.

I'd test this concept out when you feel like you are at a crossroads for a big life decision, or even when you want to dream about a future vision of what's possible or what's next for you. It can also be used when you want to vet a decision you already made and look for holes in your process. The first time you try it, choose something that is moderately important to you; that way, you can do a trial run and see what needs to be adjusted without a catastrophic ending. What's important to note is that you don't want to choose a decision that has too *low* stakes, such as the pizza toppings you want to have tonight. These little details can often become an argue-fest and are not worth your time. But your next car purchase, vacation spot, or team-building event may be good choices to test out. Hopefully, you can see the value in doing this for the big decisions, like hiring team members, buying a new house, or getting married (or divorced).

Once you've been through a few rounds, notice if there is an opinion you typically lean towards. Also, you are free to add or remove members based on the changing needs of your world. If, over the years, you met a mentor whose opinion you truly admire, add them in! Family dynamics shifted? Change away. Just don't fire someone because they have an unpopular view. There's info there too.

See the reference guide at the end of the book or visit my website for a sample Life Leadership Team and a blank template: (http://www.livefullcoaching.com/book-buyers/).

Another team member you may want to have on your LLT is your Future Self. We are going to take a journey now to meet your Future Self and see what's possible.

Meet Your Future Self

Imagine you are standing on a beach listening to the waves and feeling the breeze on your face. Your hands are on your hips, eyes closed, head tilted slightly back as the sun warms your skin. The waves crash against the shore and mist gently over you. It is a refreshing contrast to the heat of the sun.

You hear inviting music nearby. You open your eyes and start to walk against the breeze in the direction of the music. As you approach the area, you see a person sitting alone at a high-top table under a pavilion. There's no one else around. As you walk up and under the roof and into the shade, you see someone familiar. There's something about them that brings a smile to your face, and you realize with surprise it's you — a future you ten years older.

They smile back and invite you over. What can you read about them before you even take a seat at the table? Notice how they look and what they are wearing. What do you recognize that is the same as well as what is most different? Take in the essence of this future you beyond the physical features. Notice how you feel being around them.

You walk over and greet each other warmly. What happens during this greeting? How are you feeling at this point?

Your Future Self asks you if you'd like to know about your shared life ten years from now. You gladly agree, and they open their laptop where a slide show is ready to go. You see video clips and pictures of your home, places, people, events and activities. What is significant about what you are seeing? What has changed? What is the same, if anything? How are you supporting yourself? How do you spend your days? Who is in the photos and videos?

Your Future Self would like to give you a piece of advice. What is it they say, and what is it about? You'd like to know about how to get to where they are now. You ask what is one thing you could start doing more of and one thing to stop doing. What do they say? What else would you like them to share?

As your time together draws to a close, your Future Self sends you off with a loving embrace. You both express gratitude for the time spent together, and you walk away back to the ocean path that led you here. Your footprints have since been washed away but you find you are less lost than ever before.

Now your experience on the beach is fading away, and you are reappearing here and now in this time and space. Take a minute to write down as much as you can remember about the visit, trusting you'll recount all that is most important to you.

One of the most wonderful benefits of the Future Self exercise is that the Future Self is now part of your team. They are another "virtual coach" to tap into whenever you are stuck. I ask myself, "What would my Future Self do in this situation?" The answer is always clear, simple and grounding.

Since your Future Self has already landed the plane after journeying through at least the next ten years, what have you learned from meeting them that's important to you? How are they (you) the same? How are they (you) different? Unless you have a clear plan about where you want to end up, or how your life will evolve, there are usually some good insights from this exercise to include when you do things like vision boards. Vision boards are a visible representation of your goals that are created from pictures, magazine clippings, inspirational quotes or other materials that when gazed upon help remind you of who and where you want to be. It is best to put them in a place where you can see them frequently, like a bedroom or office wall, so that you can start and end each day with inspiration. I often take a picture and keep it on my phone or computer wallpaper so that it is a portable, feel-good vision as I navigate my day.

The Utopian Life Description

I hired a home organizer who was also a Feng Shui practitioner, and I learned from her about the bagua. The Chinese translation of bagua literally means "eight areas." It is used for analyzing your energy in your home, office, garden, or other locations. While the bagua does not overlap perfectly with my Wheel of Life, both concepts are quite aligned. The categories include things like family, travel, helpful people, children, creativity, wisdom, fame, career, wealth, relationships, and health. I like to look at this and compare it with the Wheel to be sure all areas are covered when designing a vision board. You can view a bagua at my website: (http://www.livefullcoaching.com/book-buyers/).

We learned earlier that your inner game of your thoughts and feelings drives the best actions. This is why we are taking the best of the Wheel of Life, TRAMS, the bagua and our feelings to create a Vibration Vision Board.

Let's take a look at why this is important. Often, when we dream big or actually play big, there can be feelings of resistance that creep in. A personal example for me is the idea of winning the lottery. I like to play, and I enjoy the idea of scoring all of those numbers for the big payoff, but too much "found" money actually brings me anxiety. I have so much resistance about it because it steps on some of my values and beliefs. I have a high work ethic, and I believe in earning your wealth. I have also created a story that I will be judged and resented if I win the lottery.

Now, I can do all of the work that I'm teaching you in this book to shift that story. However, for me, it's more important to honor my values of creation and freedom through growing my business and making a difference in the world with my God-given talents, so my energy and feelings are more aligned with that. My vision board does not include winning the lottery, but yours may and can! What it does include is elements of wealth-creation that honor one of my values, freedom, on my terms. When you look at the elements of the vision board, you should feel energized. Even the eustress that I mentioned earlier is a positive energy. These high-flying vibes do not mean they are easy, it just means you are more elevated and will attract more of what you want.

I was quite familiar with designing and reviewing job descriptions after being a manager and in HR for many years. When I first started my vision board, I took a huge poster board and wrote "Utopian

Life Description" at the top. I loved the holistic view of my entire life, so I used the Wheel of Life as the template. I then used sticky notes to brainstorm, since I like to change my mind. Each pie slice had elements that were important to me, including things like daily workouts and naps, income goals, vacation destinations and home improvements. As I got new and better ideas, or as goals were met, I'd take down that sticky note and revise with the new and improved goal. Over time, through more Law of Attraction experience, I realized how important the vibration or feelings related to the goals were — even more important because from there stemmed the aligned and inspired actions to meet or exceed them.

Let's look at the health section of the Wheel. If you have a goal for a race time, also include what values are honored and what feelings are represented by engaging in and/or accomplishing this goal, similar to the thrill and resonance from the TRAMS process.

Health Example:

- Goal: run a half marathon in less than two hours
- Feelings (thrill): pride, excitement, confidence
- Values (resonance): consistency, work ethic, dedication

Get creative, and allow the goals, photos, represented feelings and values on the Vibration Vision Board to call you forth to live your best life.

Please see the resource section of my website to use the Wheel of Life and other tools as you design your own Vibration Vision Board: (http://www.livefullcoaching.com/book-buyers/).

Life Purpose

It is quite common for my corporate clients to change jobs or get promotions where they've been assigned to certain roles. The company is thrilled with their performance and they want to move them around to various positions for their development, as well as the company's needs. "Things just come up for me," I hear frequently. But what about what you want independently of this prompting? Sometimes, when the offers slow down, people are left with a lull or even a mini panic about what's next for them.

Since we always want to cast a wide net around our life and be sure to gather all the pieces before considering our next role, it's a good exercise to look at your life purpose. What is your bigger agenda for why you are here on this planet, and how does a corporate role or any other role fit into that? Sounds deep, I know. We're moving straight into your soul contract. Don't fret; it doesn't need to be this intense. Just like the Future Self or other exercises that pull you out from the weeds, this, too, helps you see what's important to all of you so that you are aligned with your powerful choices.

Similar to values, we want to allow life purpose to reveal itself organically through powerful questions. Below, you'll find some scenarios that will help you to think about life purpose. As you read each one, write down your answers before moving on to the next one. I've done this live with clients before, with eyes closed or open, and there are always revelations.

Inner Journey #1

Imagine you have been given a lifetime of free ads on many media types such as TV, radio and podcasts that reach thousands of people every hour. You have the opportunity to affect these people in any way you would like. What would you say in your ad? What impact does your message have on the receivers? Take a few minutes to journal your experience and answers.

Inner Journey #2

Imagine you are sitting at your own funeral or "celebration of life" service. People are telling stories about their experiences with you and how you've made a difference in their lives. Who are the people in the room? What do they say to you about the impact you've had on them? Take a few minutes to journal your experience and answers.

Inner Journey #3

Imagine you are the first person to reach Earth after traveling from light years away by spaceship. There is no one here yet, and the land, culture, and "politics" are all a clean slate from which you can create anything. What's the most important thing you want to see established here? What role do you play? Take a few minutes to journal your experience and answers.

Inner Journey #4

Imagine that, upon waking up, you find you have a superpower. With this newly anointed power, you can change just one group of people and give them all the same gift. Who is it that you help? What is the gift that you give them?

Reflect back on what came to you during these inner journeys. What were the themes? What is unique to you in creating all of this? What is your urge? How did your contribution make you feel?

Life Purpose Statement

An optional exercise for you (but one I find to be very impactful) is to create a life purpose statement from all of your themes. When going through coach training at CTI, it took me many weeks to finally crystalize mine, but I was happy I figured it out.

The ultimate goal is to come up with the metaphor that fills in the blanks of the following statement: "I am the ___(metaphor)___, that ___(has impact in the world/on others)___."

When I was going through this, I knew I was some sort of energy. I tend to zap in and out with my thoughts and words, sparking all kinds of fires. This is my gift. I landed on the following statement that has since inspired my style, brand and business logo and has rung true for me ever since: "I am the lightning that changes the world one strike at a time."

Having these Higher Self-perspectives on your life will help you manage the day-to-day time-suck so differently. Through these new colored lenses, what do you notice isn't as important as it was 24 hours ago? What is more important?

In the next chapter, we will revisit all of the learnings we've discussed so far and explore some other skills to authentically connect your whole life with your leadership at work. When you play a bigger game in life, it often seems like there are either people or circumstances (or both) that remind you to stay safe and small. I'm here to tell you that it's serving *them* more than you when these forces come your way.

Think of this as a big test, perhaps the biggest in your life up to this point. We've all been through struggles and tragedies. My guess is that you haven't gotten this far in life living on Easy Street or having everything unfold perfectly for you. And, if you have, I'm surprised you've read this far in the book!

CHAPTER 10
LEADERship

In this chapter, you will be reminded of potential pitfalls and be grounded in traditional leadership skills that will help all of the internal work you've done up to this point come to life in your relationships at work and at home.

Your biggest obstacle, however, will likely be yourself. All of these tools and processes may sound great in print and in theory, but when it's time to apply them and shift, get ready for the gremlins to throw eggs at your new house. I teach these concepts, and still, I am the client of my own processes and need to tap into these when the going gets tough. Just like a new muscle you're trying to develop, it's important for you to train for strength of your inner game. Remember things like gratitude to combat the longing and the wanting.

When you find yourself getting upset with your progress (or lack thereof), remember to be grateful for your awareness and be kind to yourself in the process. When your inner critic comes screaming back, remember the gifts and the redirection to get back on track. When your calendar is getting trampled on, remember your role in scheduling sacred "me time" for think-tank activities at work.

Only you can set and maintain these boundaries. And, by all means, only you can train others to help you set those boundaries, especially if you have administrative support or other advocates to help reinforce this. Say "no" to more things that drain you in order to say "yes" to things that fuel you. And when that crazy-long to-do list is keeping you up at night, take deep breaths and focus on the nanosecond — what you need right now, knowing you have permission to change your mind tomorrow. Oh, and guilt. That lovely feeling that creeps up, just when you want to do something for yourself. Remember, when you win, everyone wins!

So, let's lean into the fact that the obstacles are coming, but you now have more in your arsenal than ever before. How can all these be applied to the workplace when they feel so self-serving and woo woo?

In order to be the best leader that you can be, it pays to do the work as a whole human so that your rock-star authenticity shines through effortlessly. I often see my clients encounter this common pitfall: they are shining as the lighthouse, but others aren't in a place yet to see their brightness. Let's discuss how we get others to play a bigger game along with you in a judgment-free yet influential way.

The LEADER Method

When I facilitate a team session, one of the most important things we do at the beginning is set some rules of engagement. We do this with new client coaching relationships as well, and it is also applicable to personal relationships. Consider these the necessary walls of the sandbox or of a pool so that we can play and have a good time as we explore.

The acronym for this work is, appropriately, LEADER, and it stands for:

- **L**isten
- **E**xplore

- **A**ssume positive intent
- **D**epersonalize
- **E**ngage
- **R**esponsibility

Listen.

You may think it's ironic that the first step in wanting to influence others is to listen. Listening doesn't mean agreeing, and it doesn't mean that you've signed up for more work or a new way of thought. It just means you are allowing another's message to land with understanding. That's it. As long as you are waiting to talk or hoping the other party just zips it so that you can get your point across, you are *not listening*.

I know this is hard! We just spent all this time on inner game and being sure we are grounded in our values and what's important to us. All of this is still true. It's really just a nuanced question of timing. When you are truly listening, it's not about you just yet. It's about the sender of the message wanting to convey something and be heard. This is a key to progressing to some sort of assertiveness or common ground.

If you think this only matters at work, guess again. This will be the hardest thing to do well with those who are closest to you. Your relationship with your spouse, child, or friend will improve and be more fulfilling when you actively listen to what's on the other side. We will get into more skills for active listening in a bit.

Explore

Exploring means experimenting with the unknown and having an open mind. If we are right all the time and know all the answers, what is there to learn? Remember when we discussed curiosity versus judgment. As long as you've made up your mind, the growth stops. Exploring and experimenting are important guidelines so that you and your partner, team, or family can create the best outcomes.

Assume Positive Intent

This one, all by itself, is a game-changer. When you hold the space for positive or even neutral backstories, there will always be a better outcome. Take, for instance, an example in which someone does not respond to an email you send. If you assume that person doesn't like you or doesn't care, then you'll be stewing while you wait for the reply. But maybe it went to spam! Maybe they didn't read it yet. I'm not asking you to make excuses for people. I'm saying that, by assuming positive intent, you won't get yourself needlessly worked up about something. Again, you'll find the evidence for whatever story you have in your head, so make it a good one.

Depersonalize

I get the most negative feedback from people in marketing about this one. In this case, "depersonalize" just means that it's not always about you. For example, you may receive negative feedback, or someone may tell you about an opportunity to do something differently with your team. By engaging in some of the first few rules like listening, exploring, and assuming positive intent, you'll learn that the message is usually about the sender, not you — even when it seems to be about you!

For real: don't take the bait. Detach and depersonalize to see the pain the other person is in and leave the defensiveness at the door in order to get to higher ground. It's not a competition unless there are two people competing. If you have any doubts about this one, don't worry — we will dig into it further when we discuss how to manage conflict a bit later.

Engage

Be present. Do your part. Put the phone and laptop down at home or in meetings. Stop multi-tasking and give your full attention to whatever or whoever is in the space. Be on time. Regardless of how you chose to participate, you will always play a role in what's co-created, so you might as well engage and get your needs met also.

Responsibility

With any experience, you get what you put into it. This is true for both meeting participation and personal relationships. Responsibility also relates to the intention, not the expectation. For example, you may argue that you put more into your marriage or meeting preparation than the other party, so you didn't get back what you put it. I'm inviting you to look at what you own and what you are responsible for. Responsibility is like a karma boomerang: you get what you give.

Focus on your energy and your perspective. For example, have you ever been to a training where you were skeptical of the concept being taught? Perhaps you were sitting there with your arms crossed and a prove-it-to-me smirk, digging your heels in as the content was delivered? At the end of the training, you said "what a waste of time that was." Well, you can see how your perspective drove that outcome. Had you intended to learn and be a champion of what was unfolding, your experience would have been different. Leave the victim mentality at home and own how you show up mind, body and spirit.

The LEADER acronym is the standard way I start meetings and also invite other participants' rules of engagement. The goal of LEADER is to create a fruitful and safe environment. Usually, confidentiality enters the rulebook, as well as anything else that helps people play a bigger game. I'm not re-inventing the wheel of communication skills. There are plenty of books and online sources out there about listening, assertiveness, and conflict management. So, now I want to provide some of the insights I've learned over the years so that you have them in one place as you continue to weave your leadership quilt together.

Levels of Listening

Have you ever been in a conversation or an argument when the other party says, "I hear you, but…"? Insert your "ugh" and eye-roll. It's very dismissive to hear that in the heat of a discussion or even a benign dialogue. You can *hear* people in the background — nature sounds or noises, too — but doesn't mean you are *listening*. To truly listen is another skill called active listening.

Why and when do you find it hard to suspend your inner chatter and really listen to someone else? There are many roadblocks to becoming a good listener. I'm sure a few come to mind for you. Think about what was happening when you couldn't be this wonderfully Zen and receptive being. In full honesty, I find it hardest to listen when I don't like someone very much, when I'm not in a neutral-feeling place, when I'm short on time, or when I'm in the middle of something that's important to me. Here's a list of some typical frequent offenders for listening well.

- Time: bad timing, not enough time, differences in time zones
- Dialect, accents, etc.
- Energy level
- Varying opinions, judgments or perspectives
- Tone or volume
- Lack of interest in the content
- No personal connection
- Competing priorities

Whatever it is for you, know that awareness is the first step to overcoming these hurdles, just like everything else. Being able to ward off heavy conversations when these roadblocks are around is key for when you do finally engage in a dialogue.

For example, have you ever been right in the middle of pulling a presentation together, and someone does the "drive by" and asks if you have a minute? We all know it's never really a minute, but you want to be approachable and say "yes" anyway. Maybe you keep typing while they are talking to you, or you sit stiffly, secretly resenting their need because you have a deadline waiting for you back at the laptop.

What you can say instead that honors both of you is, "You matter and so does this topic. In order to give you my full attention, we'll need to meet after 3 p.m. when I can be more present. Does that or another time work for you?" Of course, the specifics will vary, but what stays intact is the respect you are offering to them and to yourself.

CTI introduced me to three levels of listening: internal, focused and global.

Internal listening is the chatter in our heads that we hear. This can be quite the distraction when you are attempting to focus on the needs of the other party. Often you are half-listening in this case because of the conversation you are having in your own head.

Focused listening is when you are hanging on their every word and nothing else around you matters. These are pretty intense conversations, to the point where even the fire alarm isn't disturbing you. This could also happen during a dinner date when you want your attention to your loved one to be undivided.

The third form of listening is *global,* and this encompasses all of the sights, sounds, and all-arounds of the conversation. Take into account the words, the tone, the body language, even the energy of what's happening in the environment. We use the latter in coaching quite a bit when it seems like something is an interruption, but it's actually quite perfect to weave it into what's happening.

One time, during a coaching call, the client's dog was barking and playfully engaging with his owner. Rather than pretend that wasn't happening, I listened to the new sound and asked how this playfulness of the pup relates to our topic. What wisdom does this dog have for us right now? Hence, global listening involves us all dancing together.

Now, let's talk a little bit more about active listening. Active listening has a "look" about it, or a posture. You may have heard of the SOLER method developed by Gerard Egan. SOLER stands for:

- **S**quare posture
- **O**pen
- **L**eaning
- **E**ye contact
- **R**elaxed

When you square up, all of your energy is facing the person. Openness means you are receiving the message. If you can try this right now in a chair, cross your legs and your arms, hunch over and fold your chin to your chest. Say the words, "I am open!" How does that feel? The odds are that your words and body language are not in the same zip code. Try changing this: By leaning forward, you become engaged in the conversation. They say that eye contact is the window to the soul, and it's true: it is an important tool for connection. However, be careful not to eyeball someone with too much intensity — instead, assume the relaxed state we strive for.

There are other aspects of listening, such as the head nod and other non-verbal clues, which tell the speaker you are plugged in. One of the best tactics in active listening is to use *the replay method*. Here, you replay the actual words, the emotions you are witness to, or anything behind the words that you are feeling. This is where global listening comes in.

Another active listening skill is *the pull*, or "tell me more" statement. There's always more than the first statement that comes out of the speaker's mouth. Case study: any moody tween on the planet. When you ask, "what's wrong?" you are typically met with the answer "nothing."

When you say, "tell me more about that," you begin to peel back the layers of the onion. At work, you may encounter a disgruntled employee who says they are ready to quit. You can probably imagine how the words "tell me more" or a similar tactic will get more details on the table.

The benefits of active listening are mutual. The person speaking will eventually be disarmed once they know you fully understand where they are. And you win because you now have information and a receptive person on the other end of the conversation. Together, you can get somewhere better than if you both were just talking at each other.

Assertion

Sometimes I get asked, "At what point is it my turn?"

When you ask if it's okay for you to share your point of view, then it's time to talk and get your needs met. Assertion is when you have a need and you are confident that it is time to ask for it and act on it.

There is an assertion continuum that shows assertion as shades of grey vs. black and white. On a scale of 1 to 10, there are three ranges: 1 to 3 is passive, 4 to 7 is assertive, and 8 to 10 is aggressive. As Colleen Kelley writes in *Assertion Training: A Facilitators Guide*, the following behaviors are exhibited in each range.

The passive, or non-assertive, person does the following:

- allows themself to be interrupted, subordinated, and stereotyped
- has poor eye contact
- has poor posture and defeated air
- withholds information, opinions and feelings
- is an ineffective listener
- is indecisive
- apologizes, avoids and leaves

The assertive person does the following:

- states feelings, needs, and wants directly
- has good eye contact
- has straight posture and competent air
- is able to disclose information, opinions, and feelings
- is an effective listener
- initiates and takes clear positions
- confronts with skill

The aggressive person does the following:

- interrupts, subordinates and stereotypes others
- has intense and glaring eye contact
- has invading posture and arrogant air
- conceals information, opinions and feelings
- is an ineffective listener
- dominates
- is loud, abusive, blaming and sarcastic

When you read these behaviors, where do you think you naturally fall most of the time? Of course, you may have certain tendencies that differ from situation to situation, but odds are you have a dominant operating style. The awareness is important so that you can course-correct if need be to be more effective. Yes, I want you to be authentic. And if you are not getting what you want consistently, which is what assertiveness is, then you aren't winning either.

Watch for the passive tendencies in your behavior; they aren't always as easy to identify. The other person may throw you the "I'm fine" or "it's fine." I liken that to the other F-word. "Fine" is a trap! In almost all cases, the other person is not fine, they're just saying that. But you won't really know it's a problem until a future blow up when nothing's fine, and the dissertation of all of the wrongdoings they've been hanging on to spills out. It's really unfair all around, so if this sounds like you, I will give you the mad lib here to get in the game with your needs sooner.

I invite you to Play it Straight with this professional mad lib. You may have seen it as the three-part I statement based on the Gordon Model by Thomas Gordon, Ph.D.

Playing it Straight

Part 1:

- When you ... (insert objective example)
- I feel ... (insert emotion)
- because ... (insert your value stepped on)

Part 2:

- Therefore, what I need is … (behavior change or request)
- because … (insert your value you want honored)

I'd like to note that in Part 1 that you can replace "I feel" with "the impact on me is." This is helpful primarily for women or any situation when we've been told to keep feelings at bay. The intention is the same, and often the receptivity is higher.

This is a very respectful and assertive way to give feedback and request that something change. No matter how much we pout, people cannot read your mind. This is very helpful to remember when dealing with the people closest to us.

Here's an example of playing it straight at work: "When you are consistently late for meetings, the impact on me is lost productivity, and that is frustrating for me. Therefore, my ask of you is to make this a priority and be here on time, so that we can respect everyone's time and agenda."

And here's an example of playing it straight at home: "When you don't show up for dinner, I feel disappointed and worried because I value family time and thought something was wrong. Therefore, next time call me and let me know you are not coming home, so that I can manage expectations and adjust to keep the family aligned."

Just because you ask doesn't mean you are going to get what you want. But the odds of you getting what you want without asking are slim anyway. This is where conflict management comes in.

Conflict Management

When people hear the word "conflict," they think it's always this heated battle. Conflict just means misalignment. I often use this term when coaching clients when they aren't sure how to give feedback to a boss or subordinate without triggering them. A simple "hey, can we chat so that we are aligned?" is a good lead-in.

Here is the TNT process: Transparency, Not Triangulation. Be transparent to the person directly about what/how you feel and your perspective. Triangulation involves a third party solving it for you, and you definitely do not want to go that route. It happens all too often, and it's a powerless place to be. You deserve to be respected and to respect others. The best way to handle situations like this is directly, with confidence, and in person. Phone and video can also work due to remote locations and global roles, but in person is best. Do not engage in conflict management via email or text due to the one-way nature and the challenge of interpreting tone and meaning.

Not everything warrants this big candor fest. When there's a conflict, or a misalignment, you have choices. The Five A's help you consider your options. They are as follows:

- Address (you address it one-on-one)
- Alter (your views, your situation, etc.)
- Accept (really — this doesn't mean just nodding your head and stewing silently)
- Act victimized (not really a good choice; may show up in triangulation or passive/aggressive behavior)
- Avoid (not a powerful choice either, shows up as passive behavior)

When you choose to address conflict, assert with respect — and do so with the TEAM acronym in mind.

TEAM

- **T**ransparency: acknowledge there is a problem (use the three-part "I" statement about emotional impact and needs).
- **E**xplore: listen to what's happening on their side, pay attention to the issue, emotion and needs.
- **A**ssess: what are the possible solutions and respective impacts based on both sides' needs and wants?
- **M**eet: get to common ground, negotiate, contract, re-contract. How will you proceed? (e.g., bring in a mediator or unbiased 3rd party, decide actions/follow-ups, when/if to escalate, etc.)

These processes all start from your inner game and good intentions. When the timing or situation is such that you are not in a good place mentally, your outcome will be less desirable. It is best to get aligned with yourself first before attempting to get aligned on the outside. It is no different than what we've addressed earlier in the book! (The T-tool is a good way to do this). If your inner game is dialed in, then you will have a better experience and likely an aligned outcome that supports both you and the greater good.

The moment you dive in on autopilot and allow overwhelming and reactive emotions to rule you, you've just drained your energy. It's okay to have bad moments, hit the reset button and try again. Before each interaction, tap into one or more of the many tools we've reviewed up to this point. You can find downloadable versions at my website: (http://www.livefullcoaching.com/book-buyers/).

CHAPTER 11
"THRIVEABILITY"

You picked up this book because you didn't have enough time in your day. Work was getting the best of you, and you were second-best for your family and yourself. You wanted to love the balance that you created in your whole life — including at work and at home. Now, let's review all of the steps and tools we've covered so that you do choose to powerfully move forward toward making your dreams come true. In this chapter, we'll weave all of the lessons from the book together; you will understand that we don't arrive anywhere on this journey, but rather continue the cycle of what I call "Thriveability." Let's look at next steps and how to continue to give you the support to amp up your fulfillment.

I see you, and I know you all too well. I was you, and I'm also married to you (meaning, my husband is a living example of this!). I honor your work ethic and how stuck you feel sometimes when it's all piling up around you. There is so much good here. And, in order to get out of your own way, one needs the awareness to name it — whether that stems from a wake-up call like I had, or a slow churn on the way to burnout.

The struggle is real. But understanding your pain scale, triggers, and working through them in real time buys you the needed space to think and choose your life. Allow yourself to feel it and identify where your body is holding your stress. Then, take inventory of your whole system using the Wheel of Life, which helps you address the wonderful, dynamic human being that you are.

Then, you focus on all inner-game work. You realize that, in order to create the time and life you desperately want, you need to focus on that inside job. By shifting the power from your ego and inner critic(s) to gratitude and powerful choice, you are able to claim your power back. Forgive yourself for feelings of failing, guilt, or righteousness. Instead, when you chose to heal, you bring peace to the whole process. Practicing tools such as the T-tool will help with your intention that is within your control and releasing the expectations that are out of your control. This puts the power back where it belongs — with you.

Identifying, harnessing, and honoring your values are the North, South, East, and West of your inner GPS. Your value clarification and decision making will inform your conception of a fulfilled life, including your desire for time, love, money, health and so many other things.

Dealing with and setting healthy boundaries with your inner critic, limiting beliefs, guilt, and any energy suckers creates more sacred space for you. Purposefully say "no" to perspectives and actions that drain you in order to say "yes" to new ways of thinking and supportive behaviors that fuel you. Practicing healthy boundaries will shift the balance of power in your favor. I have provided you with some tools and tactics to make this more real for you, such as TRAMS, goal setting, calendar blocking, the Self-Care Calendar and other exercises to apply as you put the inner game into outer game practice.

Remember, you are not alone. Perhaps the most useful tool and team member of all, your Higher Power, is here to help you succeed. In order to keep that inner game alive, focus on how to vibrate with how you want to be to create more of the same. Your "to be" list creates inspired actions. And the ability to delegate to the Universe or God is such a gift. Tapping into this inner guidance through breath, mindfulness or meditation creates more allowing and receiving, something you may be in dire need of in your world of business and ticking clocks that never stop. The guidance is always there, you just need to slow down and get quiet to hear it.

Tools such as the Vibration Vision Board and the Law of Attraction all help you to create and design your best life. When you connect with your Future Self and get more clarity on your Life Purpose, you are better able to seed your dreams and inspire future actions. Your Life Leadership Team will never fail in steering you in the right direction when combined with your inner GPS. In the end, you still have the freedom to decide how you use these tools, but now you are better equipped to do so unapologetically with more alignment and authenticity than ever.

When we crossed the bridge to bringing this to your corporate leadership, we reinforced the skills of LEADERship: listening, assertion, and conflict management. Thus, we are able to help bring people along with the new bar we've set for ourselves. As a reminder, the roadblocks will pop up, but now you can handle them like the boss you are.

My wish for you is that you are no longer waiting until the mythical start or finish line to be happy. We are in a cycle of "Thriveability." You will be experiencing evidence of energy shifts and more powerful decisions that lead to a better use of how you spend your minutes, hours, and days. You are encouraged to continuously evaluate your choices based on your inner game and then choose again. You've been taught how to spot setbacks and deal with them in real-time. By maintaining a cycle mentality, you'll lose the expectation of arriving and feel more fulfilled during this journey.

So, what is next for you? You have everything in this book to be successful along with the resources and the downloadable links available to you at my website: (http://www.livefullcoaching.com/book-buyers/).

These tools are gifts to bust through burnout and support your "Thriveability" cycle.

If you are finding that you want to be guided through this process first-hand, I'd love to support you! Keep me posted on your success and your hiccups so that we can work through it and keep you moving towards the balance you wish to create in your whole life.

My clients view me as a champion and part of their "Thriveability" cycle. Many are repeat clients — or have never let me go for the past several years. It's not because they aren't 100 percent capable, but rather they understand the value of having an expert parachute in to help them see who they really are and support what they really want. It's like having a catalyst on tap vs. a dependency of a crutch. Having a coach in your world to mirror what's needed to help you grow is a wonderful gift. I always have my own coach (or coaches) for this very reason.

So, please reach out if you want to work one-on-one together. We can work this book and apply it directly to your life to experience sustainable, immediate, and unapologetic change to create the balance you are seeking in your career and your whole world. Your Future Self will thank you, and you deserve to be the client of your own awesomeness.

Thank you for being here! I'm honored you made time for it and for YOU.

RESOURCES

1. All resources are available at: (http://www.livefullcoaching.com/book-buyers/).

2. **Tools & Worksheets**
   - LFC Wheel of Life
   - Saboteur Worksheet
   - Values Matrix
   - T-Tool
   - TRAMS Worksheet
   - Self-Care Calendar and Instructions
   - Life Leadership Team
   - LEADERship
   - Vibration Vision Board

3. **Apps**
   - Breethe
   - Calm
   - Mindful Mynah

4. **Books**
   - Co-Active Coaching, New skills for coaching people towards success in work and life. Second Edition. Whitworth, Laura; Kimsey-House, Karen; Kimsey-House, Henry; Sandahl, Phillip. Mountain View, California Davies-Black Publishing, 2007, https://coactive.com
   - SOLER reference: Egan, G. (1986) The Skilled Helper. A Systematic Approach to Effective Helping, 3rd edition. Belmont, CA: Brooks/Cole
   - Abraham-Hicks Books: (http://www.abraham-hickslawofattraction.com/books.html)

ACKNOWLEDGMENTS

Thank you, God, for allowing me to show up in a powerful way on this planet. Anything other than giving you props is E.G.O. (Edging God Out, per Wayne Dyer. Thanks, Wayne!)

I want to thank my parents, Cecilia Campbell and Anthony Graziano, for always supporting me, showing me stellar work ethic, how to be a survivor in the worst of times, how to respect our fellow humans, and for being there for me no matter what.

Mom, you taught me what raw strength and vulnerable love look like. To take the good and blow the rest away. That we are all children of God. I love you with my heart and my soul. Your love is unconditional, and you are my person.

Dad, you taught me so much that I'd need one of your calculators to tally it all. I'll forever be grateful for our sweat equity no matter what we fixed together. As you say about life, "at least we are on the right side of the grass."

To my husband, Nick, thank you from the bottom of my heart for allowing me to jump when I saw a light so bright, I couldn't ignore it. Your support of me being Chief Possibility Officer was mission critical to creating a life we love for us and our family, as well as the lives I impact through my work and this book. I love you dearly, FB.

Thank you to my children, Olivia, Ray and Elizabeth, for being my biggest reasons to be a better human being. You are my greatest teachers. I want to be a good role model for you, even through the ugly mistakes and the raving successes. My biggest wishes for you are to do no harm, take no sh*t, and shine your loving, divine light for yourself first with God in your heart and then world will benefit from it.

For my sister, Nicole, thank you for always dancing with me in this life even if we mess up the words to the songs. Our hearts want to do good in this world, and that's one great thing to have in common. I love you.

To my niece, Lea, thank you for being here to celebrate my milestones and for believing in me. I love you.

For my brother, Tony, who left this world way too young, thank you for showing me how to live fully from day one. I'm grateful for our brief but powerful time on this planet together. Only the good die young.

I am so grateful to all of my coaches and teachers throughout the years who have helped me embrace my potential, my voice and my talents in this life. Among the many influencers who I'd like to thank are: Sensei Dane Sutton, for teaching me that the time to strike is when the opportunity presents itself. Bob Gamgort, for seeing the coach in me way before my time and for valuing that role for years since. Stephanie Yost, for being my first coach and role model for how life coaching really impacts a soul. To the Coaches Training Institute for showing me how to transform lives while I transform myself.

Thank you to all of my family, friends, and colleagues inside and outside my corporate career who have been a part of my journey to mold me to who I am up to this point. Without the highs and lows, I would have never known for what to strive, how to grow and play a bigger game.

And last but not least, I am so grateful for my clients who mirror back to me exactly where the growth is needed for them, for me and for the greater good. It is such a pleasure to do this work, and you give me the gift of that every day. Thank you dearly!

ABOUT THE AUTHOR

Janine Graziano-Full is a fiercely committed executive life coach who guides corporate professionals toward choices that create a deeply fulfilling life they love. She is the CEO of her whole world, including Live Full Coaching, LLC, her family and farmette, where the challenges of work life balance mirror those faced by her client base. She is a sassy and soulful professional who understands that while all of these roles in life can be overwhelming, it is possible to feel in control and have space in your day for the things and people you love.

Janine has over 24 years of corporate experience as of this printing — 14 years inside as a corporate executive in various functions and the remaining years outside as an executive life coach and team facilitator in full service of the corporate warrior. What lights Janine up about this work is that she knows you don't have to change jobs, skip sleep or vacations, or wait until you retire to have a deeply fulfilling life you love. She has been working with hundreds of amazing clients with similar worries and concerns as you and guiding them to achieve remarkable success.

Janine's path to become a corporate life coach became clear during her Human Resource and Talent Management experiences when she was exposed to executive coaches who focused solely on the functional needs and not the whole human before them. At the same time, she personally felt burned out and wanted to take her life back. Janine hired a coach outside of work to understand the process of life and career transformation as well as to become that catalyst for other executives. She left her corporate world as a trained and certified coach through the Coaches Training Institute and stepped fully into championing executives from the outside as their executive life coach.

A few things about Janine and her experience that might surprise and delight you while serving your work together:

- She loves the Law of Attraction and helping you manifest energetically what you desire.
- She holds a fourth degree Black Belt in Isshinryu, is a CrossFit Level One Trainer, and has participated in numerous competitions, running races, triathlons, marathons and Tough Mudders.
- She is a Reiki Master and practices daily on her husband, three children, plants, pets and willing clients.
- Her life purpose statement is "I am the lightning that changes the world one strike at a time."

It would be her pleasure to guide you to achieve the results you desire and the life you imagine in your coaching together.

Website: http://www.livefullcoaching.com

Email: Janine@livefullcoaching.com

Facebook: Janine Graziano-Full Page

LinkedIn: Janine Graziano-Full

THANK YOU

"If you think you are leading, but no one is following, then you are only taking a walk."
— *John C. Maxwell*

Thank you for taking this walk with me. I'm so happy you took the time to read this and to put yourself first for once — or at least for a change. Be kind to yourself as you start to claim your power back and make choices for a more fulfilling life.

If you are in need of a partner to help you live your best life, a life by your design, then I invite you to reach out to me. I'd love to hear from you via email or social media about what questions you have, what roadblocks you are facing and what successes you are experiencing. As your coach, I will be your champion to help you create the life you love at work and home.

Wishing you an unapologetically-balanced life, one powerful choice at a time!

Much love and gratitude,

Janine

Made in the USA
Middletown, DE
19 November 2020